CRIMINAL
INVESTIGATIONS

HOMICIDE

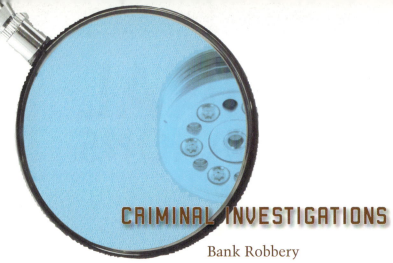

CRIMINAL INVESTIGATIONS

CRIMINAL
INVESTIGATIONS

HOMICIDE

RICHARD WORTH

CONSULTING EDITOR: **JOHN L. FRENCH**,
CRIME SCENE SUPERVISOR,
BALTIMORE POLICE CRIME LABORATORY

CHELSEA HOUSE
PUBLISHERS
An imprint of Infobase Publishing

CRIMINAL INVESTIGATIONS: Homicide

Chelsea House
An imprint of Infobase Publishing
132 West 31st Street
New York NY 10001

Library of Congress Cataloging-in-Publication Data
Worth, Richard.
Homicide / Richard Worth ; consulting editor, John L. French.
p. cm. — (Criminal investigations)
Includes bibliographical references and index.
ISBN-13: 978-0-7910-9409-9 (alk. paper)
ISBN-10: 0-7910-9409-X (alk. paper)
1. Homicide. 2. Murder. 3. Homicide investigation. 4. Evidence,
Criminal. I. French, John L. II. Title. III. Series.
HV6515.W67 2008   364.152—dc22
                2008014587

Text design by Erika K. Arroyo
Cover design by Ben Peterson

Cover: Police investigators examine the remains of a body
near Kennedy Airport in New York on June 29, 1993.

Printed in the United States of America

Bang EJB 10 9 8 7 6 5 4 3 2 1

This book is printed on acid-free paper.

All links and Web addresses were checked and verified to be
correct at the time of publication. Because of the dynamic nature
of the Web, some addresses and links may have changed
since publication and may no longer be valid.

Contents

Foreword

In 2000 there were 15,000 murders in the United States. During that same year about a half million people were assaulted, 1.1 million cars were stolen, 400,000 robberies took place, and more than 2 million homes and businesses were broken into. All told, in the last year of the twentieth century, there were more than 11 million crimes committed in this country.*

In 2000 the population of the United States was approximately 280 million people. If each of the above crimes happened to a separate person, only 4 percent of the country would have been directly affected. Yet everyone is in some way affected by crime. Taxes pay patrolmen, detectives, and scientists to investigate it, lawyers and judges to prosecute it, and correctional officers to watch over those convicted of committing it. Crimes against businesses cause prices to rise as their owners pass on the cost of theft and security measures installed to prevent future losses. Tourism in cities, and the money it brings in, may rise and fall in part due to stories about crime in their streets. And every time someone is shot, stabbed, beaten, or assaulted, or when someone is jailed for having committed such a crime, not only they suffer but so may their friends, family, and loved ones. Crime affects everyone.

It is the job of the police to investigate crime with the purpose of putting the bad guys in jail and keeping them there, hoping thereby to punish past crimes and discourage new ones. To accomplish this a police officer has to be many things: dedicated, brave, smart, honest, and imaginative. Luck helps, but it's not required. And there's one more virtue that should be associated with law enforcement. A good police officer is patient.

Patience is a virtue in crime fighting because police officers and detectives know something that most criminals don't. It's not a secret, but most lawbreakers don't learn it until it is too late. Criminals who make money robbing people, breaking into houses, or stealing cars; who live by dealing drugs or committing murder; who spend their days on the wrong side of the law, or commit any other crimes, must remember this: a criminal has to get away with every crime he or she commits. However, to get criminals off the street and put them behind bars, the police only have to catch a criminal once.

The methods by which police catch criminals are varied. Some are as old as recorded history and others are so new that they have yet to be tested in court. One of the first stories in the Bible is of murder, when Cain killed his brother Abel (Genesis 4:1–16). With few suspects to consider and an omniscient detective, this was an easy crime to solve. However, much later in that same work, a young man named Daniel steps in when a woman is accused of an immoral act by two elders (Daniel 13:1–63). By using the standard police practice of separating the witnesses before questioning them, he is able to arrive at the truth of the matter.

From the time of the Bible to almost present day, police investigations did not progress much further than questioning witnesses and searching the crime scene for obvious clues as to a criminal's identity. It was not until the late 1800s that science began to be employed. In 1879 the French began to use physical measurements and later photography to identify repeat offenders. In the same year a Scottish missionary in Japan used a handprint found on a wall to exonerate a man accused of theft. In 1892 a bloody fingerprint led Argentine police to charge and convict a mother of killing her children, and by 1905 Scotland Yard had convicted several criminals thanks to this new science.

Progress continued. By the 1920s scientists were using blood analysis to determine if recovered stains were from the victim or suspect, and the new field of firearms examination helped link bullets to the guns that fired them.

Nowadays, things are even harder on criminals, when by leaving behind a speck of blood, dropping a sweat-stained hat, or even taking a sip from a can of soda, they can give the police everything they need to identify and arrest them.

In the first decade of the twenty-first century the main tools used by the police include

- questioning witnesses and suspects
- searching the crime scene for physical evidence
- employing informants and undercover agents
- investigating the whereabouts of previous offenders when a crime they've been known to commit has occurred
- using computer databases to match evidence found on one crime scene to that found on others or to previously arrested suspects
- sharing information with other law enforcement agencies via the Internet
- using modern communications to keep the public informed and enlist their aid in ongoing investigations

But just as they have many different tools with which to solve crime, so too do they have many different kinds of crime and criminals to investigate. There is murder, kidnapping, and bank robbery. There are financial crimes committed by con men who gain their victim's trust or computer experts who hack into computers. There are criminals who have formed themselves into gangs and those who are organized into national syndicates. And there are those who would kill as many people as possible, either for the thrill of taking a human life or in the horribly misguided belief that it will advance their cause.

The Criminal Investigations series looks at all of the above and more. Each book in the series takes one type of crime and gives the reader an overview of the history of the crime, the methods and motives behind it, the people who have committed it, and the means by which these people are caught and punished. In this series celebrity crimes will be discussed and exposed. Mysteries that have yet to be solved will be presented. Readers will discover the truth about murderers, serial killers, and bank robbers whose stories have become myths and legends. These books will explain how criminals can separate a person from his hard-earned cash, how they prey on the weak and helpless, what is being done to stop them, and what one can do to help prevent becoming a victim.

John L. French,
Crime Scene Supervisor,
Baltimore Police Crime Laboratory

* Federal Bureau of Investigation. "Uniform Crime Reports, Crime in the United States 2000." Available online. URL: http://www.fbi.gov/ucr/00cius.htm. Accessed January 11, 2008.

Introduction

As the story of Cain and Abel in the Bible suggests, homicide has occurred in every society, beginning in the ancient world. In 44 B.C., for example, Roman senators murdered Julius Caesar because they feared that he wanted to make himself the king of Rome. During the twelfth century, murder struck the court of King Henry II in England when the Archbishop of Canterbury, Thomas Becket, was murdered in Canterbury cathedral. In the American South before the Civil War, plantation slaves killed an overseer named Duncan Skinner. In more recent times, newspaper headlines regularly contain stories of murder.

Human beings kill for a variety of reasons, including passion, revenge, anger, and greed. Although murders occur in every modern nation, the United States has the highest homicide rate: 5.9 homicides per 100,000 people. Experts believe that this murder rate may result in part from the high mobility of American society, leaving some people feeling isolated or unappreciated. A few of them may try to assert themselves and achieve a sense of importance by committing murder. Guns, the most common murder weapon, are also easy to obtain in the United States. Finally, the brain chemistry of killers combined with their childhood experiences—child abuse, for example—may influence their decision to commit homicide.[1]

Beginning in the nineteenth century, towns and cities began to create police departments to protect citizens from violence and to capture criminals who had committed homicide. Murder investigations became more sophisticated as police developed methods of analyzing fingerprints at crime scenes and conducting ballistic tests on murder weapons to help them catch killers.

By the end of the twentieth century, these investigation procedures had become even more elaborate. Currently, after a murder is committed, an investigation team photographs the scene of the crime, gathers fingerprints using special powders, collects trace evidence—strands of hair and fibers from clothing—takes impressions of tire tracks and shoe prints, and collects blood samples. These are later analyzed in the crime laboratory for clues that might lead to the murderer. DNA testing of blood samples, for example, is especially helpful. Since almost every person's DNA is unique, comparing blood found at a murder scene to a national database of DNA samples may help investigators identify a killer.

An examination of the murder victim also reveals useful clues that aid in a homicide investigation. The temperature or stiffness of the body may help determine the time of death. An autopsy may reveal a tattoo that can help identify a victim; an examination of the skin may uncover marks, such as rope burns on the neck, that could indicate the method the murderer used to commit the crime; while food found in the victim's stomach may help establish when the murder was committed. In addition to evidence uncovered in the laboratory, investigators also question witnesses who may have been in the vicinity of the crime at the time of the murder. They may be able to identify suspects and place them at the scene of the homicide.

All of this information often leads investigators to a suspect who is charged with murder and brought to trial. If the investigation team has done its work effectively and the evidence is convincing, a jury will find the suspect guilty of homicide.

Homicide:
As Old as Civilization

The Book of Genesis in the Old Testament of the Bible tells the story of Cain and Abel, the sons of Adam and Eve. According to Genesis (Gen. 4:2), "Abel was a keeper of sheep, but Cain was a tiller of the ground." Each brother made a sacrifice to God: Cain brought some of the crops he had grown, while Abel offered up a lamb. "And the Lord had respect unto Abel and to his offering. But unto Cain and to his offering," Genesis says, "he had not respect" (Gen. 4:5). As a result, Cain became very angry with God and jealous of his brother, killing him. God, of course, knew what Cain had done but when asked about it, Cain denied knowing anything about Abel's whereabouts. "Am I my brother's keeper?" (Gen. 4:9) he asked. In response, God became extremely angry and drove Cain out of his farmlands, banishing him to a lifetime of wandering. God also put a mark on him, the so-called mark of Cain, a mark of protection so that others would not kill him.

HOMICIDE IN THE ANCIENT WORLD

As this story indicates, homicide—the act of murder—is as old as civilization itself. Human beings are driven by strong emotions such as anger, jealousy, and passion, which become so overwhelming—at least in some people—that they commit violent acts. In the ancient world, Hammurabi, the king of Babylonia (1792–1750 B.C.) developed a great code of laws that enumerated many types of crimes and their punishments. Among these was homicide,

Italian baroque painting of the killing of Abel and the banishment of Cain. *Geoffrey Clements/Corbis*

which was punishable by a heavy fine or even death. The fact that homicide was included in the long code, which ran for 3,600 lines of writing etched on a tall obelisk, indicates that the King of Babylonia recognized homicide as a serious problem that had to be dealt with under the law.

Detail of Hammurabi receiving the Law from sun god Shamash on the *Stele of Hammurabi. Gianni Dagli Orti/Corbis*

Homicides also occurred in ancient Rome. Among the most famous was the murder of Julius Caesar by a group of Roman senators in 44 B.C. Caesar was a popular politician with a large following among the Roman people. He had served as consul and Pontifex Maximus, the high priest of Rome. He was also a celebrated military leader who had fought pirates in the Mediterranean and defeated a powerful alliance of local tribes in Gaul (present-day France). Following his victories in the Gallic Wars, Caesar marched on Rome and, early in 44 B.C., proclaimed himself a dictator for life. This angered the Roman senators, who saw their own power and the institutions of their republic being destroyed by Caesar.

Led by Marcus Brutus, one of the senators, they decided to assassinate Caesar. According to Nicholas of Damascus, a historian at the time, the "conspirators never met openly, but they assembled a few at a time in each others' homes."[1] First, they had to decide where the assassination should take place. Some favored attacking Caesar while he was walking along one of his favorite streets in Rome, others favored an assault on him while he was attending a contest of gladiators, but they finally decided to assassinate him when he came to the Roman Senate.

On March 15, 44 B.C.—the Ides of March—Caesar prepared to visit the Senate chambers. His wife Calpurnia begged him not to leave the house: "[she] was frightened by some visions in her dreams, clung to him and said that she would not let him go out that day," according to Nicholas of Damascus. "But Brutus, one of the conspirators who was then thought of as a firm friend, came up and said, 'What is this, Caesar? Are you a man to pay attention to a woman's dreams?'"

Caesar agreed with Brutus and left his home to go to the Senate. Outside the Senate chambers, he met some Roman priests making sacrifices who warned him about evil omens surrounding his visit to the Senate. Caesar's friends begged him to return home, but once again he ran into Brutus, who persuaded him to come inside the chamber. There, Caesar was surrounded by the group of conspirators, who at first seemed to be paying homage to him. But they "quickly unsheathed their daggers and rushed at him. . . . Everyone wanted to seem to have had some part in the murder, and there was not one of them who failed to strike his body as it lay there, until, wounded thirty-five times, he breathed his last."[2]

Julius Caesar was not the only leader to be murdered at this time. In the years just before his death, Caesar had become the master of the Mediterranean world. Among his greatest conquests had been Egypt, a rich source of wheat, grown along the Nile, which was used to make bread to feed the Roman people. While he was in Egypt, Caesar had fallen in love with the Egyptian queen, Cleopatra, who had accompanied him to Rome in 46 B.C. Following Caesar's death, Cleopatra immediately headed back to Rome to defend her kingdom. Caesar had expected her to rule jointly with her brother, Ptolemy XIV, but he disappeared soon after Cleopatra returned to her capital in Alexandria. Historians believe that the queen had ordered his murder so she could rule alone. Homicide had occurred in the past among the Egyptian royal family when a contender for the throne wanted to remove a rival. The ancient historian Josephus wrote that Cleopatra had her brother poisoned, a common method of murder among the Egyptian royal family. The assassins were rarely punished.

MURDER IN THE CATHEDRAL

Among the most dramatic murders in European history occurred in 1170 inside Canterbury Cathedral in England. King Henry II had named Thomas Becket the Archbishop of Canterbury eight years earlier. Born in 1118, Becket was the son of a well-to-do merchant who had also served as sheriff of London. Educated in Paris, Becket later was named an assistant to Theobold, the reigning archbishop and the most powerful Catholic leader in England. Soon afterward, Becket met King Henry II, who apparently took an instant liking to him and eventually named him his chief minister.

King Henry was eager to gain control over the English Catholic church, which owed its allegiance to the pope in Rome, not the King of England. When Theobold died in 1161, King Henry appointed his

♀ PUNISHMENT FOR MURDER

Punishment for murder varied in the ancient world. Under the Persians during the fifth century B.C., a man who killed another might be whipped as many as 200 times. Or he might be pierced with a sharp stick and executed. In Rome, a person who committed murder might be beheaded, thrown off a cliff, drowned, burned to death, or forced to go into the Roman forum to defend himself with a sword against professional gladiators. In the United States today, murderers are executed by lethal injection, electrocution, hanging, firing squad, or gas chamber.

friend, Thomas Becket, the new Archbishop of Canterbury. The king expected Becket to work with him to increase the power of the monarchy over the church. One way that the king hoped to enlarge this power was through the courts. Previously, if a priest committed a crime, he was tried by a church court. In 1163 a priest was accused of murder and King Henry insisted that the man be tried by the government's law courts. Much to the king's surprise, Archbishop Becket opposed him, and a struggle broke out between the two men over the independence of the Catholic Church in England. Becket even went so far as to excommunicate two other bishops who supported the king.

King Henry became so infuriated with Becket that he supposedly yelled at a gathering of his government leaders, "What sluggards, what cowards have I brought up in my court, who care nothing for their allegiance to their lord. Who will rid me of this meddlesome priest?"[3] Four knights of the realm, taking King Henry literally, left for Canterbury, where they began looking for Archbishop Becket. Eventually they trapped him inside Canterbury Cathedral and began striking the defenseless Becket with their heavy swords until they killed him. King Henry was so upset at the murder that he banished the knights from his court and went to Canterbury, where he "donned a sack-cloth walking barefoot through the streets . . . while eighty monks flogged him with branches."[4] But it was too late to save Becket.

CRIMES OF PASSION

Homicide also occurs among husbands and wives whose love turns to hatred. In 1824 Fanny Sébastini, the daughter of a famous French general, married the Duke de Choiseul-Praslin at a glittering marriage ceremony in Paris. The young couple was passionately in love and during the next 17 years they had nine children. But over time their relationship became more and more strained, as Fanny became extremely overweight and grew increasingly demanding. The duke could not cope with her and lived apart from his wife in their enormous mansion.

Meanwhile, the couple had hired a new governess—a beautiful young woman named Henriette Deluzy-Desportes—to supervise the care of their children. Instead of spending time with his wife, the duke preferred the company of the governess and his children.

As Mademoiselle Deluzy-Desportes wrote, "Our gaiety and high spirits gave him pleasure without demanding any effort of him."[5] Meanwhile, the duke prohibited his wife from joining in this merriment, increasing Fanny's hatred of her husband and the young governess.

Conflict between the married couple erupted often, and sometimes ended in acts of violence. One night when the couple was on a vacation, the duke "chased her [his wife] from the hotel into the night."[6] The duchess accused her husband of having a sexual relationship with Mademoiselle Deluzy-Desportes and tried to obtain a divorce. The duke was stunned and humiliated because divorce was almost unheard of in nineteenth-century France.

Apparently, at this point the duke decided to seek his revenge against the duchess by murdering her. He planned to sneak into his wife's bedchamber on the ground floor of their home during the middle of the night and unlatch a door that opened to the outside. The duke hoped that this would suggest that an intruder had committed the murder. At about 4:00 a.m. on August 17, 1847, he quietly entered his wife's bedroom, tiptoed up to her bed, withdrew a knife, and began to slit her throat. The duchess leapt out of bed screaming and began running around the room, trying to get away from her husband. But the duke struck her again and again, and finally broke her skull with a candlestick. The duchess was already dead when police were finally called to the scene.

Although her husband claimed that an intruder had entered the house and killed his wife, the police found the duke's nightclothes burning in the fireplace in his bedroom. He had tried to remove any evidence of his wife's blood, which had splattered over his clothes, by setting fire to them. The police also discovered a pistol the duke had carried when he had entered his wife's room. It was lying under her corpse—obviously, he had overlooked the weapon and forgotten to take it with him. This was an early example of crime scene investigation. The police arrested the duke and brought him to prison to stand trial for homicide. But, unable to face the humiliation of a trial, he took arsenic poison and died six days later.

HOMICIDE IN THE UNITED STATES

This murder-suicide of a French noble couple in 1847 caused a sensation in the Paris press. Ten years later, newspaper accounts told of an equally brutal homicide—this time in Natchez, Mississippi, a town located on the Mississippi River in the United States. Natchez was settled by the French in the eighteenth century, and became part of the French colony of Louisiana. The territory was purchased by the United States in 1803, becoming an American territory through the Louisiana Purchase. During the nineteenth century, cotton plantations sprang up in this area of the South, and Natchez became a prosperous river port where cotton was loaded onto steamboats for shipment to textile mills in the North.

Among the elite members of Southern society were well-to-do plantation owners who controlled vast acres of fertile land, which was worked by African-American slaves. To supervise the work of the slaves, the Southern aristocrats hired overseers—men who were responsible for making sure that the slaves worked hard to bring in a bumper crop of cotton each year. Among these men was 37-year-old Duncan Skinner, overseer on the 900-acre Cedar Grove plantation, located a few miles southeast of Natchez. Skinner supervised the work of approximately 80 slaves, at least until May 14, 1857. On that day, according to historian Michael Wayne:

> It was just after breakfast when the slaves first reported that Duncan Skinner was missing. . . . By late afternoon some of his friends became alarmed and organized a search. A little while later they came upon his horse wandering along the road, riderless, its saddle pulled loose. But it was past midnight when, guided by torchlight, they finally found the body of the overseer. It lay sprawled across the exposed roots of a beech tree, no more than a half-mile from his cabin, in a strip of woods running along the edge of the plantation.[7]

At first it appeared that Skinner had fallen off his horse, hit his head (a wound was found on his temple), and died accidentally. But further evidence called into question the original verdict of accidental death. Skinner had supposedly gone hunting, but he had not taken his favorite saddle, nor was he carrying the powder container or shot bag necessary to fire his gun. In addition, a substantial sum of money had mysteriously disappeared from his home.

During the era of slavery in the South, plantation owners—the most powerful men in most regions—formed committees to investigate crimes, especially if there was any suspicion that slaves might have committed a crime. Following Skinner's murder, 18 white men, led by Alexander K. Farrar and David P. Williams, formed a committee to investigate the overseer's death. Farrar and his men began rounding up some of the slaves on the plantation and questioning them. When they spoke to Jane, one of the cooks, she was so frightened that she immediately confessed that a homicide had indeed been committed. Jane implicated three slaves named Henderson, Reuben, and Anderson.

During questioning, Henderson told Farrar that he and the other two slaves had snuck up on the overseer's cabin during the night. Upon entering the house, they attacked Skinner. Although the overseer had tried to escape, the three slaves were more than a match for him and beat him over the head until he fell to the floor. Then they brought Skinner to the woods, where Reuben broke his neck—the blow that finally killed him. Afterward, the slaves removed Skinner's bloodstained clothes and dressed him in a set of clean clothing that they had brought with them. Then they put his body next to the tree and left his horse nearby. All the evidence initially pointed to accidental death. Further questioning led the men to the money taken from Skinner's cabin, which had been hidden away by another slave named Dorcas.

Why had the slaves committed the brutal murder? Was it for the money or had there been another motive? According to Michael Wayne's research, the reason had not been Skinner's money. Many overseers on plantations treated slaves harshly, according to Wayne, and some slaves refused to put up with this treatment. They ran away from plantations and lived in nearby swamps, which plantation owners were reluctant to enter. Others escaped along the Underground Railroad, which were secret routes that those opposed to slavery established to rescue slaves and take them to the safety of the North. Murders of overseers also occurred on some Southern plantations. Apparently, Skinner was extremely brutal and beat and abused the slaves. According to Wayne's research, they killed him in hopes that someone less cruel would take Skinner's place. Indeed, John McCallin, a friend to the slaves, had told them that he planned to marry Cedar Grove's owner, a widow named Clarissa Sharpe, and take over the plantation. After the marriage, McCallin promised to improve the slaves' lives on the plantation, but he never carried out his promise.

Sometimes murderers seek revenge by killing someone who has wronged them, but the victim may also be someone completely innocent who has done the murderer no harm. In the early morning of November 15, 1959, Richard Hickock and Perry Edward

MURDER IN MADISON SQUARE GARDEN

By the beginning of the twentieth century, Stanford White was one of the most famous architects in America. The architectural firm of McKim, Mead and White had designed numerous homes for wealthy clients, monuments such as the Washington Square Arch, and public buildings including Madison Square Garden, an enormous entertainment center in the heart of New York City. When he wasn't at work, the handsome, red-haired White was a regular on the New York party circuit, often accompanied by a string of beautiful, young women. One of these women was Evelyn Nesbit, who had appeared in the musical show, *Floradora*, and whose portrait had been painted by renowned American artist Charles Dana Gibson. One man described Nesbit as the "loveliest looking girl who ever breathed."[8] Early in her teen years, Nesbit had developed a relationship with White that continued until she was 19. After their romance ended, Nesbit met Harry Thaw, the heir to a huge manufacturing fortune, and agreed to marry him.

Thaw was a brute of a man who regularly beat Nesbit, but she seemed willing to put up with the abuse in return for marrying into great wealth. Nevertheless, when Thaw found out about her prior relationship with White, he was enraged. On the evening of June 25, 1906, Thaw and Nesbit were attending a performance of a play entitled *Mam'zelle Champagne* at Madison Square Garden. Down in the front, near the stage, Stanford White was having dinner with some of his friends and watching the play. When the performance ended, Thaw left Nesbit and walked down the aisle to the table where White was sitting. He pulled out a revolver, pointed it at White, and shot him three times in the head, killing him instantly.

Thaw was arrested and put in jail to stand trial for murder. While this looked like a simple case, Thaw hired a very experienced trial attorney named Delphin Delmas who came up with a plan to save his client from execution. Delmas decided to plead

Smith entered the home of Herbert Clutter, a well-to-do farmer in Holcomb, Kansas. Smith and Hickock had met while they were locked up in the Kansas State Penitentiary for check fraud and theft. Believing that Clutter had large amounts of money in his

Thaw not guilty by reason of insanity. According to Delmas, Thaw said he had heard voices in his head that had ordered him to shoot Stanford White. Meanwhile, Thaw's lawyer portrayed White as an immoral man who had seduced Evelyn Nesbit when she was still a young girl. The jury found Thaw innocent by reason of insanity. That is, they believed that Thaw's mental condition at the time of the murder prevented him from knowing that he was doing something wrong. This was one of the early cases where the insanity defense was used and where it was also successful. Thaw was committed to the New York State Asylum for the Criminally Insane, and Evelyn Nesbit went back on stage, earning the huge sum of $3,500 per week—about $81,000 today.

Harry K. Thaw (left) and Stanford White (right). *Bettmann/Corbis*

Eugene Hickock (left) and Perry Smith (right) were found guilty of murdering Herbert Clutter, his wife Nancy, and their two children. The book *In Cold Blood* by Truman Capote is based on this murder case. *Bettmann/Corbis*

home, Hickock and Smith demanded that he produce it. When he finally convinced them that there was very little cash in his house, Hickock and Smith realized that they would be sent back to prison if Clutter and his family testified against them. So Smith blew off Clutter's head with his shotgun, and then the thieves murdered his wife, Nancy, and their two children.

The murderers fled the scene of the crime and headed first to Mexico and later to Las Vegas, where they were picked up by police, who had interviewed one of their cellmates, Floyd Wells. Wells said he had told Hickock about Clutter and the money that might be found at his home.

The murder and trial of Hickock and Smith, who were eventually found guilty and executed, became the subject of a book by author Truman Capote. *In Cold Blood*, which was published in 1965, made Capote famous. He combined the facts of the case with many of the elements of a novel to create an instant best seller. The story of homicide fascinated Capote's readers then, just as tales of murder continue to captivate audiences today.

Homicide:
The Statistics and the Causes

Known as "the beautiful cigar girl," Mary Rogers worked behind the counter of John Anderson's tobacco store in New York City during the late 1830s. Mary proved to be wonderful for business, bringing in large numbers of men who wanted to buy their cigars only from her. Then, without any warning, Mary stopped coming into work one day in 1838. By the time two weeks had elapsed with no word from her, Anderson had not only become concerned about her safety but also about the future of his business, which was rapidly declining. Then Mary suddenly reappeared with no explanation of where she had been. She worked at the tobacco shop for the next three years, and Anderson's business continued to thrive.

In June 1841, when Mary was 21, she became engaged to Daniel Payne, a local cork cutter. But before the marriage could take place, Mary disappeared once again. Three days after her disappearance, Mary's battered and bruised body was found in the Hudson River.

The grizzly murder of Mary Rogers was splashed across the front page of New York's newspapers. It also attracted the attention of Edgar Allan Poe, one of the city's best-known writers. Poe was one of the pioneers of a new type of writing—the murder mystery. Indeed, he had just published the short story "The Murders in the Rue Morgue," featuring French detective C. Auguste Dupin. Soon afterward, Poe began writing another murder story, entitled "The Mystery of Marie Roget," based on Rogers' death but set in Paris.

While some of the newspapers seemed to think that a gang of thugs had killed Rogers, Poe was convinced that she had been the victim of a single murderer. In his story, Poe wrote about a piece of cloth around her neck tied with the type of knot used by sailors and probably used by the killer to drag Mary's body along the ground to the banks of the river. If a group of men had killed her, Poe believed, they surely would have picked up Rogers' body and carried it to the river instead of dragging it.

New York police never solved the death of Mary Rogers, but the incident inspired many New Yorkers to call for reforms in the police department. As a result of a reform act approved in 1845, the department improved and became more effective not only in preventing homicides but also in finding the criminals who committed them.

HOMICIDE—THE ENDS AND THE MEANS

Homicide, a word that comes from the Latin word *homicida*, means "a person who kills another." It usually refers to murder, where the killer intended to take the life of the victim, or to manslaughter, where death was not intended.

The United States has one of the highest homicide rates in the world: 5.9 homicides per 100,000 people. In England, by contrast, the rate is 1.6 homicides per 100,000.

According to psychologist John Gartner of Johns Hopkins University, when people in a society move often, it's easy for some to feel they have no ties to their communities. Instead, they may feel isolated, alone, and sometimes threatened, and sometimes even decide to assert themselves by taking the law into their own hands if they feel they have been wronged or slighted. These feelings may increase in a society, such as the United States, with a wide gap between the wealthy and everyone else.[1] Author Sharon Begley of *Newsweek* adds:

As long ago as [the nineteenth century] observers have divined that the American character had been forged on the frontier. Far from civilization and the reach of laws, we created the cult of the rugged individual who took justice into his own hands.[2]

Approximately 90 percent of all homicides are committed by males, according to Begley. Almost half of them are young men, under age 25. One reason that homicide is primarily a male crime is that men are expected to be more aggressive than women. Even among children, boys learn to defend themselves; indeed, they often believe that only "sissies" won't hit back and attack someone who seems to be pushing them around.

The means to commit murder are readily available to most people. Many items, including a blunt object or even the killer's hands, may serve as a murder weapon, but in the United States, guns, especially handguns, are the most common weapons used to commit murder. Among victims under the age of 34, approximately 70 percent are killed by guns.[3] In the United States, more people own guns than in any other nation of the world. Guns can easily be purchased over the Internet or at gun stores. Gun dealers are expected to do a brief background check on their customers to ensure that they do not have a criminal record or that they have not spent any time in a mental institution. But this does not eliminate many potential killers.

No one under the age of 21 is legally permitted to purchase a gun in the United States, but the law can easily be violated. In 1999 17-year-old Dylan Klebold and 18-year-old Eric Harris, both seniors at Columbine High School in Littleton, Colorado, marched into their school building and killed 13 people and wounded 23 others. They bought their guns from a friend who had purchased them at a gun show where no background checks were required.

A smaller number of homicides are committed with other types of weapons, such as an ax, a knife, or another sharp instrument. In 2005, for example, about 6,000 homicide offenders between the ages of 18 and 24 used a gun, while only 2,000 used another weapon such as a knife.[4]

Poison is another method that murderers have used for centuries, although it is rarely used today. In ancient Rome, the poet Juvenal mentioned the poison aconitine, which is derived from a plant called monkshood. In his *Satires*, Juvenal mentioned "its usefulness for poisoning inconvenient relatives or rivals,"[5] according to author David Owen. Other types of poison include atropine and strychnine, which are also derived from plants, as well as the metal thallium. Thallium is completely tasteless and can be dissolved in water so the victim is not aware of being poisoned. The poison, which damages the cells and nerves, produces symptoms that often mimic a severe flu, except that the victim's hair starts to fall out.

Thallium poisoning was the method used by Caroline Grills to murder her victims in Sydney, Australia, during the 1940s. Grills began by killing her stepmother, an 87-year-old woman named Christina Mickelson; then Grills murdered a relative of her husband's named Angeline Thomas; her brother-in-law, John Lundberg; and a family friend, Mary Ann Mickelson. Apparently Grills put the poison in tea, which she prepared for each of her victims. She also

Evidence in a murder case, Coca-Cola bottles tainted with thallium encased in plastic bags in a lab at a police station. A deadly poison, thallium was the preferred murder method of Caroline Grills in Sydney, Australia, in the 1940s. *Acey Harper/Time Life Pictures/ Getty Images*

began serving the tea to Lundberg's widow and her daughter, both of whom began losing their hair over the next few weeks. A relative brought some of the tea to police, which was later analyzed and found to contain thallium. Grills was arrested, tried, found guilty, and sentenced to life in prison.

Strangulation is another method that murderers use to kill their victims. In 1889 Michel Eyraud and his girlfriend Gabrielle Bompard strangled Toussaint-Augsent Gouffé. At first they tried killing him with the cord from his dressing gown, "passing it over an overhead pulley, but the knot [around his neck] failed to hold. Eyraud was forced to strangle Gouffé with his bare hands,"[6] according to author David Owen. Once the man was dead, the murderers looked for the large sum of money that they thought Gouffé kept in his office, but found very little. Although the murderers put the body in a trunk, which they hid in the woods, it was later discovered. Eyraud and Bompard were eventually captured and convicted of murder.

Some murderers place their hands around the victim's throat, cutting off blood to the brain, resulting in unconsciousness and death. Other murderers use a ligature, such as a rope or cord, to commit the murder. In one killing, a man murdered his unfaithful wife with her panty hose while she was lying in bed. After the murder, he stuffed her body in the trunk of a car and drove it to a nearby parking lot, where he left it. Police discovered the car two days later, conducted investigations, and arrested the man for murder.

Murders are also committed by beatings—either the murderer uses his or her hands or strikes the victim with a blunt object such as a club. Many of these beatings occur between spouses—in a majority of cases, a woman becomes the victim of violence by her current or former husband. Each year over 1,200 women are killed by a husband or boyfriend, and some of these deaths result from beatings.

MOTIVES FOR MURDER

Robbery and greed are common motives for homicide. On July 9, 1985, Steven Benson blew up his mother in her car in front of their home in Naples, Florida. Mrs. Benson was a wealthy woman, and Steven expected to inherit her estate when she died. Then he learned that his mother was planning to change her will because she had discovered that Steven was embezzling money from her. Before his mother could change her will, Steven wired her car

JEAN HARRIS AND DR. HERMAN TARNOWER

One of the most bizarre murder stories to gain national attention involved Jean Harris and Dr. Herman Tarnower. Born in 1923, Harris had grown up in a well-to-do family outside of Cleveland, Ohio. She later attended Smith College, married her girlhood sweetheart, and the couple had two children. The marriage ended in divorce in 1965, and a year later she met Herman Tarnower.

Dr. "Hi" Tarnower was a successful physician who had started the Scarsdale Medical Center outside New York City and a notorious womanizer. Nevertheless, Harris and Tarnower became involved in a whirlwind romance, and in 1967 he gave her a large, very expensive engagement ring. But Tarnower seemed in no rush to get married; indeed, he was dating other women during his engagement to Harris. Although she continued her relationship with Tarnower, Harris grew more and more depressed. To help her deal with the depression, Tarnower wrote her prescriptions for pills. Meanwhile, he began an affair with his administrative assistant, Lynne Tryforos.

In 1976 Harris, who had pursued a long career in school administration, was named to run the elite Madeira School for girls in McLean, Virginia. But as her relationship with Tarnower grew worse and worse, it became increasingly difficult for Harris to do her job. She even began to contemplate suicide.

While Harris's depression was deepening, Tarnower had become world famous after publishing *The Complete Scarsdale Medical Diet* in 1979. Harris had worked on the book with him, but she received little credit, and Tarnower spent most of his free time with Tryforos. In 1980 Harris wrote Tarnower a long letter expressing her pain and anger over his relationship with Tryforos. Soon afterward, Harris decided to visit Tarnower, bringing a gun that she had purchased. Harris said later that she had become so distraught that she planned to use the gun to commit suicide. Driving to Tarnower's house on March 10, 1980, she arrived late

with a bomb that exploded when his mother turned the key in the ignition. The blast also killed his adopted brother, Scott. Steven was arrested and later convicted of the two murders.[7]

at night after he had already gone to sleep. Harris woke him up and the couple engaged in a heated fight over his relationship with Tryforos. During the struggle, Harris took out the gun, later claiming that she had planned to kill herself. Instead, she shot and killed Tarnower. Harris was later tried, found guilty of murder, and sent to prison.[8] She served 12 years and suffered two heart attacks while in prison. She was released from prison on December 29, 1992.

Murderer Jean Harris sitting at a table in the Bedford Hills Correctional Facility in New York in 1982. Harris was found guilty of murdering her former lover, Dr. Herman Tarnower. After serving 12 years in prison, she was released in December 1992. *Marvin Koner/Corbis*

Among the oldest motives for murder are passion and jealousy. In 1973 a beautiful model named Melanie Cain moved into a New York apartment with a successful businessman named Howard "Buddy" Jacobson. Together they started a modeling agency and hired many attractive young women. Although Cain remained with Jacobson for five years, their relationship grew steadily worse. In 1978 she met Jack Tupper, who had moved into an apartment on the same floor as Cain and Jacobson.

Tupper and Cain began going out on dates and eventually Cain decided to end her relationship with Jacobson. "Buddy" Jacobson was enraged that Cain had left him and tried to break up her romance with Tupper. When this did not work, Jacobson decided to kill him. With the help of two accomplices, he stabbed Tupper and shot him seven times. Jacobson was later arrested by police and convicted of murder.[9]

In addition to jealousy and passion, revenge is another motive that impels some people to commit homicide. Cho Seung-Hui, the 2007 Virginia Tech shooter, was an outsider who had endured years of ridicule from his classmates in high school and college. He planned to take his revenge by killing some of them. "You forced me into a corner and gave me only one option," Cho said in a videotape that he made shortly before killing 32 people at Virginia Tech and taking his own life.[10] Other murderers kill out of strong political beliefs. In 1865 John Wilkes Booth planned to assassinate President Abraham Lincoln and other members of his cabinet in an effort to save the Confederate States of America from being defeated at the end of the Civil War. With Lincoln dead and the North without its great leader, Booth seemed to believe that the Confederacy might somehow win the war, although Confederate General Robert E. Lee had already surrendered his army. On April 14, 1865, five days after Lee surrendered, Booth carried out the assassination, shooting President Lincoln as he watched a play at Ford's Theater in Washington, D.C.

Other motives for murder include greed. In 1879, for example, Kate Webster, employed as a servant to Julia Thomas, a London widow, killed her employer, stole her jewelry, and sold it. More recently, rival drug dealers and their gangs battle each other for control of the illegal drug market where vast sums of money are at stake. As a means of eliminating their competitors, these gangs regularly resort to murder. They also murder witnesses who have agreed to testify against them.

PROFILES OF KILLERS

Many people are motivated by greed, passion, or revenge, and some may even be suffering from mental disease, but they do not commit homicide. Only a relatively small number of individuals actually commit murder. Studies by Adrian Raine, a professor at the

♀ MURDER AND INSANITY

Historians often speculate about the mental stability of a fanatic like John Wilkes Booth. Clearly, some killers are insane at the time they commit a homicide. In 1843 Daniel M'Naghten tried to assassinate British Prime Minister Robert Peel at his home in London. Although the Prime Minister had never spoken to him, M'Naghten was apparently convinced that Peel and others were involved in a plot to kill him. As a result, M'Naghten went to Peel's home, but, instead of murdering the prime minister, mistakenly shot and killed his secretary, Edward Drummond. At his trial, M'Naghten's lawyer produced expert testimony showing that the defendant was not aware that he was committing a crime. M'Naghten believed that he was only defending himself. The judge agreed and M'Naghten was confined to a mental institution.

Following the case, the so-called M'Naghten Rule began to guide courts and juries as they tried to determine whether a killer could be found not guilty by reason of insanity. According to the M'Naghten Rule, which is still used today, a killer suffering from mental illness might not really know what he was doing, might be unable to control his actions, and might not realize that they were wrong. Consequently, he would not be guilty of murder.

On July 7, 1986, Juan Gonzalez boarded the Staten Island Ferry in New York with a concealed sword. Soon afterward he began slashing passengers aboard the boat, killing two of them before a retired policeman finally stopped him. Claiming that God had told him to commit the homicides, Gonzalez was evaluated by psychiatrists who said he was unfit to stand trial. He underwent treatment and a new trial was ordered in 1988. Gonzalez admitted to the homicides before the trial began, but claimed to be suffering from "mental disease and defect" at the time. Therefore, he was placed in a mental health facility for long-term treatment.

University of Southern California, show that some killers have a reduced level of activity in the areas of the brain that control impulsive behavior. "This is the part of the brain that says, 'Let's stop and think about this again,'" Raine explains. "It has a calming effect on the emotional regions of the brain that give rise to pent-up anger and rage." Without this calming effect, killers may act impulsively and commit murder. Reduced activity "also means that empathy will be off."[11] As a result, killers feel no compassion for their victims and are more likely to take out their aggressions by resorting to violence. However, this does not excuse the fact that they take the lives of innocent victims and they should be punished.

Some of these killers may have been raised in homes where they were victims of child abuse or where they witnessed violent behavior by one parent toward another. As a result, they grow up believing that violence is a normal method of dealing with problems. A child who is too weak to fight back against a powerful parent or a child who is bullied in school may take out his or her anger on others—first, against other children and later, as the child grows up, against other adults. A long-term study of men in New Zealand found that those with a specific gene that produces low amounts of an enzyme called MAOA are more likely to be highly aggressive. But this was only true if the men had been abused as children.[12]

In other words, no one factor creates a killer, but rather a combination of biological makeup, life experiences, and cultural factors can all contribute to create an individual who commits murder.

The Police and Homicide Investigations

Brother Cadfael—the fictional creation of mystery writer Ellis Peters—was a highly successful detective who lived at the monastery of St. Peter and St. Paul in Shrewsbury, England, during the twelfth century. Before becoming a monk, Cadfael had been a Crusader in the Holy Land as well as a sailor on a fishing boat. Along the way, he had also acquired a broad knowledge of human nature as well as become unusually skilled at using medicinal herbs to cure a wide range of diseases. Cadfael lacked the services of a crime lab or DNA testing that investigators use today and instead had to rely on his knowledge and common sense to solve crimes. In *Monk's Hood*, for example, Cadfael was confronted by the sudden death of Gervase Bonel at Shrewsbury Abbey. Bonel was the husband of a woman named Richildis, whom Cadfael had known many years earlier. By smelling the breath of the dead man, Cadfael concluded that he was poisoned by aconotine, derived from the plant monkshood, which the monk kept in his laboratory. This information helped Cadfael save an innocent man and eventually find the killer.

EARLY POLICE FORCES

The state of homicide investigations and police work during Cadfael's time was not much different than it had been over a thousand years earlier. In ancient times, when a murder was committed, it was usually up to the family and friends of the victim to track down the killer and bring him or her to justice. It wasn't until the first century B.C. that Roman emperor Augustus established the first police force. Known as Vigiles, there were 7,000 of them in Rome who patrolled the streets at night looking for fires. They carried buckets of water, which they used to douse house fires whenever they broke out. At the same time, the Vigiles also kept a lookout for burglars and other criminals who might be preying on innocent citizens. Due to the success of the Vigiles in Rome, similar groups were set up in other Roman towns to serve as policemen.

During Cadfael's time, murder investigations were often the responsibility of the local English constable or sheriff. Selected by a powerful member of the nobility, the constable was in charge of organizing a hundred families in his area to deal with a crime. People were summoned by the constable, or even by a private citizen who issued a "hue and cry" if a murder had been committed. They might yell "Murder!" or "Stop thief!" following the commission of a crime. In response, a group of people in the area was organized to go after the suspected criminal. The king appointed *Shire reeves*, or sheriffs, as the chief law enforcement officials of English counties, or shires. Indeed, Cadfael often relied on the local sheriff to organize a few men and capture the criminal who the monk believed had committed homicide.

By the eighteenth century, London had become a heavily populated city and it was no longer practical to rely on groups of people called out by "hue and cry." Instead, Londoners who had been the victims of a crime hired men called "thief-takers," and paid them a reward to hunt down the criminal. Among the best-known thief-taker was Jonathon Wild. Wild, however, was later charged with making deals with the thieves he was supposed to capture and selling the items they had stolen. He was jailed, tried, and finally hanged in 1725.[1] Thief-takers provided a valuable service throughout London. Henry Fielding, a local magistrate (law enforcement official) and well-known novelist, organized them during the 1740s (Fielding had taken over the magistrate's office at Bow Street in London.) From his headquarters, he directed the so-called Bow Street Runners, a group of thief-takers. As soon as a local resident reported a crime, Fielding sent the Runners out to find the criminal and paid them a reward for capturing them.

In addition, Fielding and his brother, John, gathered information about crimes across London to help other magistrates in their jobs. "The aim of this new system," according to one historian, "was to deter criminals by increasing the certainty that they would be detected and prosecuted."[2] It became quite successful and spread to other towns in England.

During the nineteenth century, the work of the Runners was expanded as the English government put police patrols on the streets during the day and at night. This was an effort to prevent crime rather than simply going after criminals after an offense had been committed.

In 1829 Robert Peel, a prominent minister in the English government, convinced Parliament to pass the Metropolitan Police Act. This established a paid, professional police force in London, the first one in the world. Dressed in blue coats with long tails and tall hats, the men were popularly known as "Bobbies," after Robert Peel. Each carried a wooden stick, a pair of handcuffs, and a rattle that he used to summon other police officers if help was necessary to capture a criminal. The headquarters of the Metropolitan Police was Great Scotland Yard in the center of London. Scotland Yard became widely known as the center of police investigation.

EARLY TECHNIQUES OF HOMICIDE INVESTIGATION

While the English police force was becoming more professional, the techniques of murder investigation were also becoming more scientific. During the 1870s a Scottish doctor named Henry Faulds began investigating the unusual swirls and ridges that formed each person's fingerprints. Using ink, Faulds took the prints of his friends' fingers and discovered that each had a unique set of fingerprints.

Meanwhile, an English scientist named Francis Galton had been pursuing similar studies. By recording a wide range of prints, Galton had developed "a basic method of fingerprint classification based on grouping the unchanging patterns of whorls, arches, and loops, unique to every individual," according to author Edward Ricciuti.[4] In 1892 Galton published a book entitled *Finger Prints*. At first, Scotland Yard was skeptical about the value of fingerprinting, but

⚲ HENRY FAULDS AND FINGERPRINTING

Born in Scotland in 1843, Henry Faulds worked as a clerk in Glasgow and later attended medical school. In 1873 he left Scotland to serve as a Presbyterian missionary in India and Japan. He began to investigate archeological sites and noticed that pieces of pottery discovered there contained fingerprints from the potters who had created them centuries earlier. In 1880 Faulds published an article describing his investigations into human fingerprints and how they differed from person to person. He also wrote about a crime involving a stolen bottle of alcohol in a hospital. Faulds explained how he used a set of fingerprints found at the scene to catch the thief. In 1888 he told the British police at Scotland Yard about his success in using fingerprints to identify criminals, but they were not interested. As author Gavan Tredoux wrote, they "may have considered Faulds a harmless crank, an impression that might have been reinforced by his aggressive personality."[3] Faulds continued working in the field of fingerprinting and published several books and articles on his discoveries during the first decade of the twentieth century. But Faulds never received the recognition he believed he deserved as the discoverer of fingerprinting. The recognition instead went to Francis Galton, whom the English courts found more credible because of his scientific studies. Faulds later became a police surgeon and died in 1930.

by the beginning of the 1900s police had begun using fingerprints to identify and capture criminals.

Scotland Yard investigated a series of grizzly murders in 1888 in the Whitechapel section of London. A man calling himself Jack the Ripper had murdered seven prostitutes. Not only had he slashed the women's throats, he had also cut up their bodies. The careful way that the murderer had cut out his victims' organs led police to believe that he may have been a doctor. Although the identity of the Ripper was never discovered, this case in 1888 was the first use of profiling to identify a murderer.

In profiling, police try to piece together similarities among the murders in serial killings to create a picture of the killer. They analyze the way that the murders were committed, noting such things as whether the weapon was the same or the murderer tortured his victim in each case. This helps create a profile of the murderer and is a technique widely used by modern homicide investigation teams.

Francis Galton (1822–1911), best known for his work in anthropology, heredity, and eugenics, was a pioneer in the use and classification of fingerprints as a means of identification. *Bettmann/Corbis*

THE MURDER OF THE FARROWS

One of the cases that helped get fingerprinting accepted as a legitimate technique to identify criminals occurred in 1905. It involved the murder of Thomas and Anne Farrow in Deptford, outside of London. On March 27, 1905, the body of Thomas Farrow was discovered by police in his paint shop, on the ground floor of the Farrow home at 34 High Street. Upstairs, Mrs. Farrow was discovered in bed with brutal head injuries from which she died a short time afterward.

At the crime scene, police discovered two masks that had been used by the murderers as well as an empty metal box where Farrow usually kept his cash. Inside the box, they discovered a clear fingerprint. After talking to people in the neighborhood, the police arrested Alfred and Albert Stratton, who lived in the area. Both men were fingerprinted at police headquarters, and Alfred's print matched the one found on the metal box.

It was conclusive proof of the identity of at least one of the murderers, but fingerprints had never before been used as evidence in a trial. The prosecution presented Scotland Yard Detective Charles Collins, who carefully explained to the judge and jury how fingerprints could identify a criminal. Collins also pointed out that the print found on the metal box found at the murder scene matched 11 of the same characteristics of Alfred Stratton's right thumbprint. The jury was convinced, and the Strattons were convicted of homicide.[5] This landmark murder case helped establish fingerprinting as an important method of identifying criminals.

THE WIVES OF BATH

A century ago two British medical experts, Bernard Spilsbury and Sydney Smith, pioneered many of the investigation procedures that are now commonplace. Spilsbury was a pathologist—a doctor who investigates the causes of death—who solved a famous murder case in 1915 known as the "Wives of Bath."

The case involved a man named George Smith, who had been married three times and whose wives had all died in the bathtub.

Smith was charged with murder, but he was quick to point out that if he had killed each of his wives, their bodies would have revealed evidence of physical harm. These would have included marks on their throats or faces as they struggled while he drowned them in the bath. Spilsbury disagreed and to prove it he brought a bathtub filled with water into the courtroom. Spilsbury had his assistant step into the bathtub and lie down in the water. Then Spilsbury yanked her quickly by her ankles, demonstrating how easily she could have been drowned without leaving any marks on her body. The jury was convinced and George Smith was convicted.

Sir Sydney Smith, a professor of forensic medicine—medicine or science used in law enforcement—was another leading British homicide expert. Early in his career, Smith had worked in Scotland and then in Egypt, where he had established a highly successful crime laboratory. Much of Smith's work was focused in ballistics, the identification of bullets and guns.

From his extensive studies, Smith concluded that each weapon and bullet was unique. With the help of two microscopes, he could compare the bullet removed from the murder victim with one taken from the weapon suspected of being used in the crime. In 1927 Smith became professor of forensic medicine at Edinburgh University in Scotland. He had been using similar techniques

♀ PROFILER, JOHN DOUGLAS

Born in 1945, John Douglas became a member of the FBI in 1970. As a student of criminal psychology, he became an expert in developing profiles of killers. Much of his information came from interviews with murderers such as James Earl Ray, who assassinated Dr. Martin Luther King, and convicted serial killers including Richard Speck and Ted Bundy. With this data Douglas began assembling descriptions of the personalities of murderers and the way that they operated. By using this information, police investigating a crime scene could create a profile of a possible murder suspect that might help them catch the killer.

In an interview with CNN, Douglas explained how some killers reveal something about themselves just "by the way they position a body." He added that killers "leave clues at the scene."[6]

SHERLOCK HOLMES

According to author Frank Smyth, Sir Sydney Smith was often compared to the legendary fictional detective Sherlock Holmes.[7] Smith graduated from Edinburgh University, which Arthur Conan Doyle, a doctor and the mystery writer who created Sherlock Holmes, had also attended. Indeed, the Holmes character was based on one of Doyle's professors at Edinburgh, Dr. Joseph Bell, who had emphasized the importance of careful observation and deduction. Police detectives had only recently begun to use many of the techniques that Holmes used to solve murder cases. These included using fingerprints and ballistics. Holmes had also designed a method of determining whether a stain on the clothes of a suspected murderer was blood or some other brownish red substance, such as rust. In many of his cases, Holmes used his superior skills of observation to solve cases that seemed to baffle detectives from Scotland Yard, such as Doyle's famous character Inspector Lestrade.

involving two microscopes to compare fibers and hairs from a suspected killer with those found at the scene of a crime. These techniques enabled Smith to solve important murder cases.

HOMICIDE INVESTIGATIONS IN FRANCE

During the nineteenth century, French police began experimenting with many of the same techniques that were being used in Great Britain. French King Louis XIV had established the first French police force two centuries earlier, and this organization had evolved into the National Police, Sûreté National, and the Police Judiciaire, a detective force that investigated homicides. Among the pioneering detectives in France was Eugène Vidocq, who was head of the Sûreté from 1811 until 1827.

During this same period, Mathieu Orfila published his book, *Traité des Poisons*, in 1814, which described the types of poisons used in murder. In the 1880s forensics professor Alexandre Lacassagne began ballistics testing that later influenced the work of Sydney Smith.

In the 1880s Alphonse Bertillon, who worked in the police department in Paris, was developing a procedure that led to more effective identification of criminals. Bertillon recognized that the only method to identify a criminal that had been previously used by the French police was a vague description made by the arresting

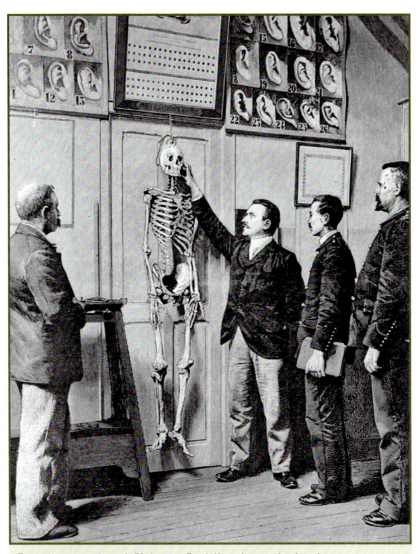

French criminologist Alphonse Bertillon demonstrates his Bertillon System of identifying criminals based on anthropometric measurements at Paris police headquarters. *Bettmann/Corbis*

PROBLEMS WITH THE BERTILLON SYSTEM

The Bertillon system involved 11 different physical measurements of an individual. Bertillon believed that the combination was unique to each person. Police departments followed this procedure and recorded the measurements of each suspect they interrogated on cards. Sometimes, however, there were mistakes and the system failed.

One such case involved Will West, who was sent to Leavenworth Prison in 1903. His measurements and physical description on his card were basically identical to those of another man by the same name of William West, who had been a prisoner at Leavenworth since 1901. Fingerprints replaced the Bertillon system because they were unique to each individual.

officer. As a result, it was impossible to be sure if someone who had committed one crime was the same person who committed another crime somewhere else. Bertillon began taking precise measurements of suspects who were brought into the police station. He measured the individual's skull, the length of the left arm, the size of the left foot, and the length of the middle finger. He recognized that the combination of these measurements was unique to each individual. Bertillon also took photographs, or mug shots, of each suspect, which were placed alongside the measurements. The Bertillon System, as it was called, vastly improved detective work, although it was later replaced by fingerprinting, which was even more reliable.

FORENSIC DENTISTRY

Another investigation technique developed in France was forensic dentistry, which involved the identification of a victim by looking at his or her teeth. On May 4, 1897, a terrible fire occurred at a society party in Paris, killing 126 people. Although police had a list of those attending the event, their bodies were badly burned and could not be identified. Finally, someone obtained the dental records of the people at the party and these were used to achieve positive identifications.

In addition to fingerprinting, mug shots, and ballistics testing, forensic dentistry became widely used in crime scene investigations during the twentieth century.

All of these procedures became part of the crime laboratory, first established by French pathologist Edmond Locard at Lyon,

Influential French criminologist Edmond Locard. *Bettmann/Corbis*

France, in 1910. Locard believed that every speck of evidence, including strands of hair or dust particles, must be collected from a crime scene and a suspect. Then this evidence must be very carefully examined and compared. Indeed, Locard's Exchange Principle became a standard for police investigations: "A criminal leaves something at a crime scene and, in turn, takes something away from it,"[8] according to author Edward Ricciuti. In other words, every contact leaves a trace.

HOMICIDE INVESTIGATIONS IN THE UNITED STATES

Police work and homicide investigations in the United States developed in much the same way as they did in Europe. During the colonial period, towns relied on sheriffs, constables, and voluntary watchmen to deal with crime and to catch criminals. As cities grew during the nineteenth century, crime also increased. In New York City, residents annually brought 10,000 cases of assault to the police department in the 1830s, but there were few murders—only seven in 1835.[9]

In an especially brutal case in 1836, a prostitute named Helen Jewett was murdered with an ax and her body was set on fire. Richard Robinson, a young clerk and a friend of Jewett's, was later arrested for the murder. He was known to be a client of Jewett's and had been seen in her room just before the murder. Robinson was acquitted, and no one was ever convicted of the crime.

In 1845 New York introduced the first paid professional police force in the United States to deal with the level of violent crime in the city. Wearing uniforms similar to the Bobbies in London, the police were known as Coppers, because they wore copper stars on their coats. Unlike the Bobbies, however, the Coppers carried guns to help them in capturing criminals. Professional police officers were also hired in other cities such as Philadelphia, Chicago, and Boston, and the police forces began using mug shots to help them identify criminals. In cities, police riding on horseback, called flying squads, were able to quickly reach the scene of a crime.

While cities and towns developed local police forces, states also created law enforcement agencies, such as the Texas Rangers. In addition, the federal government established agencies to deal with criminals, such as the Border Patrol. When the U.S. Secret Service was founded in 1865, its purpose was to crack down on counterfeit currency. In 1902 the Secret Service assumed full-time responsibility for the protection of the president, following the assassination of President William McKinley the previous year. In 1908 the Bureau of Investigation—later called the Federal Bureau of Investigation (FBI)—was established. Gradually, this organization became responsible for dealing with interstate and federal crimes in the United States, such as spying, kidnapping, and homicide.

The FBI set an example in training its agents that influenced police departments throughout the United States. The work of August Vollmer, who served as Chief of Police in Berkeley, California, from 1909 to 1932, was also important. In the past, many police officers were poorly educated, but Vollmer began hiring police officers with college degrees and established a training school for them. Many of his officers became police chiefs in other communities. In 1923 Vollmer also set up a crime laboratory that became a model for many others across the United States. Indeed, Vollmer's work helped pave the way for the types of crime scene investigations that have become commonplace in the twenty-first century.

Homicide Investigation at the Crime Scene

On the evening of June 12, 1994, police were called to the home of Nicole Brown Simpson at 875 South Bundy Drive in Brentwood, California. After arriving at the house, they saw the battered body of Ms. Brown Simpson lying in the courtyard, drenched in blood. Nearby was the body of her friend, Ronald Goldman, who had been stabbed repeatedly. Homicide detectives soon joined uniformed police. Directed by Detective Mark Fuhrman, they conducted an investigation that led them to Brown Simpson's ex-husband, former professional football superstar, O.J. Simpson. Simpson lived only five minutes away from his ex-wife. Simpson was charged with murder and went to trial seven months later.

Although the prosecution expected a conviction based on the evidence found at the crime scene, Simpson's defense team had other ideas. During the trial, they successfully cast doubt on the evidence found at the scene and the way it had been collected. For example, a black leather glove with blood from Simpson and his former wife had been found at the crime scene. Also, police had taken a sample of O.J. Simpson's blood following the murder and put it in a test tube with a preservative called EDTA. Traces of the blood, complete with the preservative, were later found at the crime scene, suggesting that police may have planted it there. Further, police had neglected to wear gloves or sterile coveralls when they arrived at the scene and, as a result, they may have brought material from other locations and contaminated the crime scene at 875 South Bundy Drive. In addition, police had used the telephone at Nicole Brown Simpson's home. As a result they might have smeared any fingerprints that may have been on it. Fuhrman had been recorded on tape during the investigation making racial remarks about O.J. Simpson. Finally, some jury members found the presentation of the DNA evidence confusing. All these factors were enough to persuade the jury to find O.J. Simpson not guilty of murder.[1]

PROPER CRIME SCENE PROCEDURES

The O.J. Simpson trial illustrates the importance of following proper investigation procedures at the scene of a homicide. If police make a mistake and the evidence is compromised, defense attorneys can cast doubt on its validity and win an acquittal for their client.

Uniformed police are usually the first law enforcement officials who arrive on the crime scene. It is essential that they not commit the same mistake that police made at 875 South Bundy Drive—using a telephone that is part of the crime scene and possibly destroying crucial fingerprints. Instead, police must be careful to disturb nothing at the crime scene. They must also control the scene by sealing it with emergency tape and creating a single method of entering and leaving the area, as well as preventing any unauthorized people, such as members of the press and curious onlookers, from being there. These people might disturb important evidence. In addition,

⎈ CHAIN OF CUSTODY

One of the most important investigative procedures at a crime scene is called the chain of custody. According to the U.S. Department of Justice, this involves the "proper documentation, collection, and preservation" of the evidence.[2]

Each time evidence is transferred from one investigator, such as a police officer, to another, such as a lab technician, the transfer should be documented. The preservation of the evidence should also be recorded. This avoids what happened in the Simpson trial, when careless evidence collection allowed the defense to call into question the integrity of the evidence.

an important function of the uniformed police is to detain any witnesses who may have been in the area when the crime was committed because their testimony may be crucial to reconstructing the homicide and eventually capturing the killer.

THE CSI TEAM

A Crime Scene Investigation (CSI) team, led by the senior investigating officer, generally conducts the investigation of a crime scene. One of the best-known teams is the FBI Evidence Response Team (ERT). It includes from eight to 50 members, depending on the size of the crime scene that is being investigated. It is larger than most local police forces, which have far less money and can afford far fewer people on their teams.

Among the ERT members is a photographer who takes pictures at the scene, a sketcher who draws the entire area including the location of each piece of evidence, a recorder who keeps a log of information from the crime scene, and an evidence collector.

The members of the CSI team should be wearing protective coveralls and gloves when they begin a murder investigation to prevent contamination of the crime scene. A team usually starts by taking a survey of the entire scene to gain a general overview of the homicide. The team looks over the scene, noting such things as the position of the victim, the condition of the location where the victim has been found, and any weapons that might be located nearby. In addition, they also begin a narrative description of the investigation, either in writing or by dictating the information into a tape recorder.

PHOTOGRAPHY

The photographer is one of the most important members of the CSI team. Photographs provide a visual record of the crime scene that can be assembled later to help investigators reconstruct the homicide and find the killer. Photographers take broad shots of various areas of the crime scene and then take pictures of each area from various angles to provide investigators with as much information as possible. Then each piece of evidence is photographed. The photographer sometimes uses a tripod to steady the camera and

Members of the FBI Evidence Response Team use shovels to examine a field near a murder scene. *Matt Rourke/AP*

ensure that the shots are as clear as possible. In addition, when size is important, a measurement scale is placed next to a piece of evidence, such as a tire track, shoe print, or fingerprint, to indicate its true size in the picture.

Each piece of evidence—such as a suspected murder weapon—is then marked, numbered, and keyed to a diagram made by the sketcher on the team. Then more photographs are taken.

The photographer uses lights to illuminate the crime scene and possibly discover evidence that may be hidden in a dark corner. For example, a cell phone from the pocket of a suspected killer may have fallen behind a large chair as the murderer fled the scene. According to the *Crime Scene and Evidence Photographer's Guide*, photographers also use oblique lighting (lighting from a low angle) "to show detail by creating shadows in the subject surface. It is commonly used when photographing . . . certain types of finger-prints."[3] Photographers also rely on special lights, such as ultraviolet, infrared, and violet light, which may reveal gunshot powder or hard-to-find fingerprints.

FINGERPRINTS

Fingerprints are pieces of evidence that generally play a crucial role in a murder investigation. Each individual's prints are different, and a single print found at the crime scene may point to the killer.

⚲ CLASSIFYING FINGERPRINTS

Investigators look for patterns in fingerprints found at a crime scene to help classify them and find a match from a database of prints. Most people have loops in their prints, which are classified as radial loops or ulnar loops. About one third of the population has whorls—oval patterns—in their fingerprints. These may be plain whorls, double loops, central-pocket loops, or accidental loops. A few people have arches in their fingerprints.

In the identification process, investigators take 10 prints—one for each finger—and then the prints are classified according to the pattern appearing on each finger. The information is then compared with many thousands of fingerprints in a computer database or Automated Fingerprint Identification System (AFIS). The database includes the fingerprints of people who have been arrested. A recovered print is then compared to all those in the

(continues)

(continued)

system. If a possible match is found, then print examiners check and double check the two prints to see if they actually match. Frequently, a single print from one finger is enough to enable the computer system to locate a match.[4]

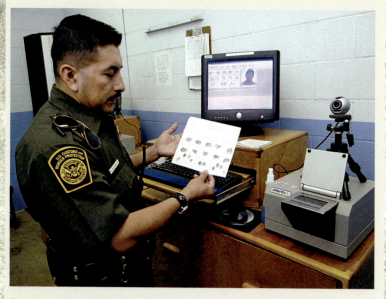

A U.S. Bureau of Customs and Border Protection agent holds a card of fingerprints printed with the Automated Fingerprint Identification System (AFIS). The computer program taps into the FBI's fingerprint database in search of a match. *Denis Poroy/AP*

Prints are formed when moisture along the ridges of an individual's fingers and palms sticks to a surface.

Prints that are easily visible are called patent prints. These kinds of fingerprints may show up on a shiny surface such as the handle of a knife, or in blood at the murder scene. Prints that are not visible to the naked eye are called latent prints. Latent prints become visible by using lights and special fingerprint powder containing chemicals such as ninhydrin and cyanoacrylate to reveal them. The investigation team dusts for prints with powder in parts of the murder scene where they are likely to appear. For example, a print may have been left on a wooden table near the body of the victim. The team uses soft brushes and a fine black and gray powder—or a metal powder applied with a magnet—that sticks to the moist prints left at the

♀ CYANOACRYLATE FUMING

Cyanoacrylate is a liquid that reacts with the chemicals in sweat to make them visible. Cyanoacrylate is regularly used to lift latent prints from a crime scene. It allows investigators to bring an item containing a latent print back to the laboratory, where it is then placed in a portable airtight chamber called a fuming chamber.

Say, for example, that a hammer is found at the scene of a murder. Although there are no patent prints on the hammer, police suspect it could have been the murder weapon and want to inspect it for possible fingerprints. After examining it for blood or other evidence, police (wearing gloves) would carefully pick up the hammer and take it to the lab where it would be placed in the fuming chamber. As the chamber heats up, the cyanoacrylate turns into a gas. The gaseous cyanoacrylate sticks to the potential latent print on the hammer and police can immediately enter the data into a computer and begin looking for a match.

A detective shows how fingerprints on a CD are illuminated using cyanoacrylate fuming. *Bob Sciarrino/Star Ledger/Corbis*

scene. After a print is revealed, it can be photographed. An investigator also places a clean piece of tape over the print, and then lifts up the print and places it on a card for the lab to examine later. In addition, investigators generally bring equipment that enables them to fingerprint any witnesses who have been detained at the scene of the crime. They also take elimination prints from anyone with regular access to the location, so that they can eliminate prints from these people. The investigator's gear usually includes printing ink, a roller, and fingerprint cards.

TRACE EVIDENCE

While fingerprints are being recovered, other members of the crime scene team are generally looking for trace evidence. Trace evidence is any evidence that is small and not readily visible on a crime scene. Examples of trace evidence include paint flecks, strands of hair, fibers (often from clothing or carpet), bits of glass, as well as blood and other fluids.

As forensic expert Paul L. Kirk wrote:

> Wherever he [the killer] steps, whatever he touches, whatever he leaves, even unconsciously, will serve as silent witness against him. . . . This is evidence that does not forget. . . . Only human failure to find it, study and understand it can diminish its value.[5]

Unfortunately, investigators failed to take samples of bloodstains at the gate to Nicole Simpson's house until several weeks after the murder, by which time the evidence had probably already been contaminated.

Investigators use tweezers to carefully remove strands of hair found at the crime scene and place the strands in plastic bags to preserve them. These hairs could be linked to the killer. In 1958 the body of teenager Gaetane Bouchard was discovered in a gravel pit in Canada. In the girl's hand was a hair follicle, which police examined in the laboratory using a process called neutron activation analysis. According to author David Owen, neutrons fired at the hair follicle "identify traces of billionths of grams of fourteen different elements in a single hair. . . . Calculations have shown that the likelihood of two different individuals having the same concentrations of just nine of these constituents is around one in a million."[6] The hair follicle was traced to Bouchard's former boyfriend, John Vollman, who was later convicted of murder.

Clothing fibers found at the scene are also removed as well as other evidence such as pieces of glass that may be from a killer entering through a window to commit a homicide. Glass samples from the scene may be compared to bits of glass found on the suspect's clothing or in his home or car.

Other investigators may be collecting soil samples or seeds in the area around the crime scene. Later, these might be matched with similar material found on a suspect's clothes or in his or her automobile. As a way of carefully examining an area, several investigators might conduct a shoulder-to-shoulder fingertip search on their hands and knees across a lawn or a small section of roadway. This intensive search may reveal a tiny piece of evidence, such as a torn segment of clothing, which might otherwise have escaped detection. Investigators also vacuum cars and crime scenes, picking up evidence that may be too small to be visible in a search.

TIRE TRACKS AND SHOE PRINTS

Bloody shoe prints led investigators up a path to the home of Nicole Simpson. Visible prints made by the soles of a shoe are usually photographed so they can later be compared with the shoes of a suspect in a murder investigation. From a single sole, investigators can sometimes gather important evidence—for example, a left sole that is more worn than a right one may indicate that the person wearing the shoe had a limp. According to author N.E. Genge:

[T]he distance between prints indicates the height of the individual. The position of feet on the floor indicate how an individual moved. . . . Depending on whether the person is running or standing or creeping, different parts of the foot strike the surface in different ways. . . . A trail of prints, even lousy prints, can lead to secondary crime scenes, to an unknown exit, to another set of prints, or to tire impressions connected to the scene.[7]

Shoe Print Comparison

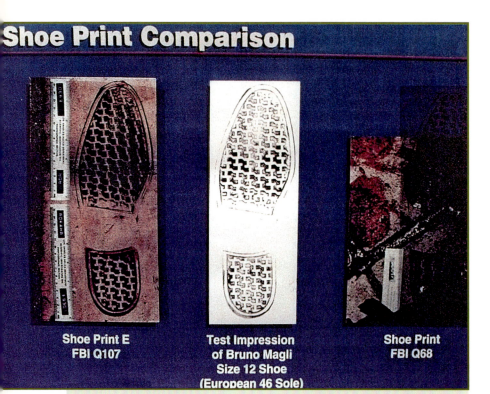

Shoe Print E
FBI Q107

Test Impression
of Bruno Magli
Size 12 Shoe
(European 46 Sole)

Shoe Print
FBI Q68

A copy photograph of exhibit 403 in the wrongful death civil suit against O.J. Simpson, which shows a test shoe print of a Bruno Magli shoe and shoe prints from the crime scene. FBI shoe print expert William Bodziak claimed to have found 18 points of similarity between shoes worn by Simpson in a 1993 photograph, shoe prints at the murder scene, and a model pair of Bruno Magli's used by the FBI for the investigation. *Susan Sterner/AP*

Investigators follow similar procedures if they discover tire tracks at the scene of a homicide. However, tire tracks must be recorded quickly because rain or snow can destroy them rapidly. Photographs are one way of recording tire tracks. Detectives also take casts by pouring liquid dental stone—like that used by dentists to take impressions of teeth—into the tire tracks. After the cast hardens, it can be removed with a print of the tire and taken to the crime lab. Then the track is compared with other tire prints in guides containing pictures of thousands of tread designs, which may lead to a match.

BULLETS AND BLOODSTAINS

Many homicides are committed with a firearm, such as an automatic pistol. In cases where a victim has been shot, investigators search the crime scene for the murder weapon. They also look for cartridge cases or bullets. The murderer may have fired more than a single bullet, and one of them may have penetrated a piece of furniture, a wall, or another object. The crime scene team carefully removes these bullets so they can be taken to the crime lab and used to identify the murder weapon.

Bloodstains at the crime scene are also invaluable sources of evidence in the investigation. DNA analysis in the laboratory can link a blood specimen to the victim, the murderer, or someone else who may have been present during the crime. Except for identical twins, each person's DNA, or genetic code, is unique. DNA profiling can be done from blood samples, as well as from samples of hair found at the crime scene. Blood may not always be easy to spot at a murder scene. Investigators use strong lights that reveal blood that cannot be seen by the naked eye. According to George Schiro, forensic scientist at Louisiana State Police Crime Laboratory, infrared film can "be used for documenting bloodstains on dark surfaces."[8] A crime scene team also uses a chemical called luminol, which is sprayed on areas in a room that they suspect contain bloodstains. The blood gives off a blue glow when the room is darkened.

To preserve blood, investigators handle blood samples very carefully. They might collect the entire item containing the blood, or carefully cut around the blood to collect only that part of the item containing it. Wet blood might also be swabbed and put into specially designed swab boxes.

Bloodstain patterns also reveal much about the crime. According to Louis L. Akin:

> The interpretation of blood spatter patterns at crime scenes may reveal critically important information, such as the positions of the victim, assailant, and objects at the scene; the type of weapon used to cause the spatter; the minimum number of blows, shots, or stabs that occurred.[9]

Suppose a victim was lying in front of a wall in a living room containing a blood spatter in the form of a mist. This is a high-velocity spatter, which usually indicates that a gun was the murder weapon. A medium-velocity spatter indicates that the weapon was a knife or club. A trail of blood may indicate that the murderer carried the victim from one place to another. It may also lead investigators to a body that has been hidden by the killer.

Paulette Sutton, an expert in blood spatter analysis, recalled the death of a homeless man that looked like an accident. However, in the room where the man had died, Sutton's investigation "turned up a bloodied table leg and bedpost." According to author Jessica Sachs:

> The impact angle of the blood spatter on the bedpost aligned with the victim's face in a way that suggested the post had been used as a weapon before being dropped to the floor, where it caught flying blood from a subsequent beating with the table leg.[10]

An accident had suddenly become a homicide. Patterns like those found by Sutton are generally recorded by a photographer so they can be more thoroughly examined later.

In addition to bloodstain patterns, investigators may also find other types of useful evidence at the murder scene. These may include marks outside a wooden door made by a tool used to forcibly enter a home. Investigators generally remove the piece of wood containing the marks. If a similar tool is later found in the possession of a murder suspect, the marks made from this tool could be compared with those found at the crime scene. Bite marks, left during a struggle with the killer, may also appear on the body of the victim. These are photographed and casts are made so they can later be compared to the dental records and X-rays of a murder suspect.

Examination of the victim also plays a key role in a homicide investigation. It begins at the murder scene and continues at the crime laboratory and the medical examiner's office.

The Homicide Victim

In 1910 the wife of Dr. Hawley Harvey Crippen, a London physician, mysteriously disappeared. When friends asked what had happened to Belle Crippen, her husband said that she had gone to the United States to visit a relative who had become ill. Later, when Belle did not return, Crippen said that his wife had become sick during her visit to the United States and died. Friends grew suspicious when Crippen was seen having dinner with his secretary, Ethel Le Neve, and she was wearing some of Belle's expensive jewelry.

Eventually, police were called in to investigate the case and finally discovered grizzly body parts hidden in the basement of Crippen's home. At first, no identification of the body could be made—at least until Bernard Spilsbury began his investigation. A small piece of skin that Spilsbury identified as part of the abdomen contained a scar that could have been made when the victim had her appendix removed. Belle had been in the hospital at one time for an appendectomy. Spilsbury also found traces of poison in the body parts.

Meanwhile, Crippen had left the country aboard a ship bound for North America, accompanied by his girlfriend, Ethel Le Neve. Crippen wore a disguise and Ethel, a petite woman, was dressed like his son. Nevertheless, the captain of the ship suspected that Crippen and Ethel might not be what they seemed. He contacted police in London and they stopped the ship when it reached its destination. There was enough evidence to arrest Dr. Crippen for murder and he was eventually convicted in a highly publicized trial.

In a homicide case the identification of a body is essential. Since homicide victims are often killed by someone they know, such as a relative, a business associate, or a friend, identification helps in tracking down possible suspects.

The process of identifying a murder victim frequently begins as soon as police arrive at the scene of a homicide. Police may learn the victim's name by questioning witnesses, or they may discover identification on the victim's body. Police might find a wallet with a driver's license or credit cards in the victim's coat or pants pocket. If the victim's shirt has been professionally dry cleaned, it may contain his or her last name, placed there for identification by the cleaners. Crime scene investigators also take fingerprints of the victim, which may lead to identification, especially if the individual has a criminal record and the prints are on file in a database.

In some cases the victim may have a tattoo or may be wearing a watch with initials on it or an unusual piece of jewelry that may lead to an identification of the body. Forensic expert Vernon J. Geberth, who was a lieutenant commander with the New York City Police Department, recalled a case where the only item left on a woman's body found in a park was a ring containing a devil's head with two diamond eyes. "The description was given to the press, with a request for anyone with information to please call the police," Geberth explained. "Twenty-four hours later we received a call, based on the description of the devil ring. A positive identification was obtained."[1]

FORENSIC PATHOLOGISTS

A forensic pathologist, or medical examiner, plays a key role in examining the victim, just as Spilsbury did in the Crippen case. A preliminary examination of the body at the crime scene may enable the pathologist to determine that the victim was killed by a gunshot or a knife. A pathologist will also gather more detailed information later during an autopsy in the medical laboratory.

One of the most important tasks of a forensic pathologist at the crime scene is to begin estimating the time of death. This information is essential in a homicide investigation because any suspect who cannot account for his or her whereabouts at the time of the murder immediately becomes a prime suspect. As the investigation continues, these suspects will be investigated to determine whether any of them had a strong motive for murder and could be guilty of the crime.

Estimating time of death involves a variety of different factors. Eight or 10 hours after death, the corneas in the eyes of the victim have already become somewhat glazed and cloudy. Body temperature is another indication of how long the victim may have been dead. Following death, the body cools from its normal temperature of 98.6 degrees Fahrenheit to the same temperature as the surrounding environment. According to Vernon Geberth, "If the body is warm, death occurred a few hours ago; if the body is cold and clammy, death occurred anywhere between 18 and 24 hours ago."[2]

Rigor mortis—the stiffening and hardening of the limbs and muscles—is another indication of time of death. This process begins about two to four hours after death has occurred and spreads completely throughout the body in about 12 hours. In about 60 hours, the rigor mortis has disappeared. The rate of rigor mortis varies, as Geberth explains:

> Obese people do not always develop rigor, skinny people develop it fast; heat speeds up the process of rigor, while cold retains it; a fight or body shock usually accelerates it; no two bodies even under similar circumstances develop it at the same time. . . . A word of caution: this factor is the poorest of the gauges used in estimating time of death because of the many variables involved.[3]

Another factor that may indicate the time of a homicide is called dependent lividity. Following death, blood begins to leave the upper part of the body and settles in the lower sections. Skin begins to turn purple where the blood has disappeared. If a victim has been lying on his or her stomach, this side of the body is purple; if the victim has been lying on his or her back, that side of the body takes on a purple color. Dependent lividity begins about one half hour after death. One way a forensic pathologist will begin to determine the time of death is by pressing on the purple area of the skin to see if blanching occurs and the skin returns to its normal color. No blanching occurs four or five hours after death, so this may help determine the time the victim died.

⚲ THE BODY FARM

Established in the early 1970s, the body farm at the University of Tennessee is one of several facilities in the United States where scientists study what happens to the human body after death. Before their deaths, some people decide to donate their bodies to the facility for research. Some of these bodies are then buried, while others are left aboveground. By examining the cadavers (bodies) scientists can learn about the rates at which bodies decompose under varying conditions. This helps in murder investigations by enabling investigators to pinpoint the time of death by examining the amount of decomposition to the victim's body.

AUTOPSY

Following an examination at the crime scene, the forensic pathologist usually directs investigators to remove the body for an autopsy. The body is placed inside a bodybag—a black or white zippered bag made of heavy plastic. Then it is taken to the medical examiner's office for a more extensive examination. An autopsy determines the cause of death (such as a gunshot wound), the manner of death (the weapon), and the mode of death (whether the victim died because of an accident, a suicide, or a homicide).

An autopsy begins with an external examination of the victim's body. A member of the pathologist's team takes pictures of the entire autopsy procedure. The pathologist also records the information gathered during the autopsy on a tape recorder, which forms the basis of a report that is written later. During the external examination, the pathologist notes the victim's height, weight, gender, the color of the hair and eyes, and the clothes he or she was wearing at the time of the murder. After removing the victim's clothes, the pathologist may discover a scar or tattoo on the victim's body, which may aid in a positive identification if one has not already been made. A detailed description of the victim's teeth may also aid in this identification. The pathologist may also find a rim burn on the victim's skin, which indicates a "wound from a weapon held directly on the skin," according to author N.E. Genge, whereas "a weapon held just a few inches back from the skin produces a noticeable pattern of soot around the wound, but no burn."[4]

A close observation of the skin often enables a pathologist to determine the mode of death. For example, police investigators may have found the body hanging from a rope tied to the ceiling and concluded that the victim committed suicide. However, rope marks on

⚲ FIXING TIME AND PLACE OF DEATH WITH INSECTS

During an examination of a murder victim, a pathologist may call for assistance from a forensic entomologist, an expert on insects. If maggots have appeared on the victim's eyes this usually

(continues)

A police officer holds up a jar of maggots, which can be used to determine a victim's time of death. *Andrew Shurtleff/AP*

(continued)

means that the murder has occurred about a day earlier because it takes this long for the eggs of maggots to hatch. In a murder that occurred outside, the victim may have eggs or maggots from a blowfly, an outdoor species of fly. A victim discovered in the woods may have eggs on his or her eyes from a housefly, which may indicate that the murder actually occurred inside and the killer took the body to the woods after the victim died. If a corpse has been left outside for many days, the type of insect found on the victim may provide clues to the time of death. For example, ants and beetles found on a decaying body indicate that death occurred from eight to 18 days earlier.

the neck may not have an "inflamed edge," indicating "burst blood vessels." According to author Richard Platt, this may indicate that the "victim was dead before hanging. This is strongly suggestive of homicide." If there is "bruising around the nose and mouth . . . [it] suggests smothering."[5]

As part of an external autopsy, the pathologist may take X-rays of the body to determine the internal location of any bullets or broken knife blades. In addition, the victim's arms and fingers are examined carefully to find out if he or she put up a struggle during the homicide. In addition, a pathologist examines the victim's fingernails and scrapes out any blood or tissue that might belong to the murderer. DNA testing of this material may lead to the killer.

Following the completion of an external autopsy, the pathologist begins an internal examination. Exploring the area under the victim's hair, the pathologist looks for head wounds that may not have been immediately visible. Using a saw and chisel, the pathologist then opens the victim's skull and removes the brain. If the victim was a baby, bleeding in the brain may indicate that the child was shaken repeatedly and harshly, possibly resulting in death. The pathologist also takes a slice of the brain for further examination. If any chemical agent, such as a poison, was the cause of death, it might show up in brain tissue.

After examining the brain, the pathologist makes a "Y" incision along the chest cavity to look at the internal organs in this area. The

? FORENSIC SCULPTORS

Sometimes a victim lies undiscovered for so long that only the skeleton remains by the time investigators find the body. To help them make a positive identification, they may rely on the skills of a forensic sculptor. These sculptors can construct a victim's face based only on the bones of the skeleton. By looking at the facial skeleton, a sculptor can figure out the general age of the victim, as well as the gender, race, and body weight. Hairs remaining on the skeleton may yield clues to the victim's hair color, which is added by placing a wig on the head.

Frank Bender is among the best-known forensic sculptors. Bender starts by photographing the skeleton of the victim. He consults a facial-tissue-thickness chart and begins creating a bust. According to *USA TODAY*, "He makes a mold of the head out of synthetic rubber reinforced with fiberglass plaster. He paints, sands and retouches the bust," until it is complete.[6]

Bender's work helped police identify the body of Frank Myers, which was found in Lancaster, Pennsylvania, in 1986, as well as the body of Rosella Atkinson, an 18-year-old girl discovered in Philadelphia in 1987.[7]

Forensic artist Frank Bender's models have helped police identify dozens of murder victims and, in some cases, find their killers.
Dan Loh/AP

heart and lungs are removed, and slices of them are taken for later examination. If ribs have been broken, this may indicate a struggle with the murderer. The pathologist follows a similar procedure with the victim's abdominal region, which contains the stomach and intestines. The contents of these organs may help determine the time of death. Food leaves the stomach about four to six hours after a victim's last meal, and leaves the small intestine about 12 hours after eating. If there is still food in the victim's stomach, death was relatively recent. However, if the stomach is empty but the small intestine still contains food, the homicide may have occurred earlier. By analyzing the type of food in the intestine, a pathologist can determine what the victim ate at a final meal.

At the completion of an autopsy, the pathologist prepares a report called a protocol, which contains all the findings of the external and internal autopsies.

Homicide Investigation:
The Suspects

In 1969 police in Austria confronted a mystery surrounding a man who had suddenly disappeared while he was enjoying a holiday in Vienna, the Austrian capital. Effective police investigation turned up a suspected murderer, but he had an alibi that seemed to put him miles away from the scene of the crime at the time of the murder. Nevertheless, Austrian investigators believed he was the murderer and collected some of his belongings to try to tie him to the crime. Among them was a pair of boots covered with mud. These were examined by a noted geologist, Wilhelm Klaus, who found that they contained pollen from a variety of trees that were only found in one location—Vienna. This was enough to tie the man to the crime, and he eventually confessed and showed police where the body of his victim was located.[1]

Finding a murderer often involves sifting through a great deal of evidence until police find the clues that bring them to the most likely suspect. Frequently, this means assembling enough details to build a convincing case. As author John Houde put it, "If it can be demonstrated that the number and type of shared details is overwhelming, then jurors usually find it reasonable to believe that two objects were once joined together."[2] These two objects may be a pair of muddy boots and a single location in Vienna.

But homicide investigators generally find their way to a suspect only after long hours of tough detective work. This usually includes talking to witnesses who may have seen something at the scene of the crime. If a murder occurred at a local park, for example, police may go house-to-house, interviewing every homeowner in the area to find out if they passed by the area at the time of the crime. Perhaps someone saw a man fleeing from the park soon after the body was discovered. A witness's description often leads police to someone they think might have been involved in the crime, sometimes based on a prior criminal record.

To verify the identification, police conduct a line-up. A group of at least eight similar-looking people are placed in the line-up and the witness is asked to identify the person he thinks he saw leaving the scene of the crime. But what if the suspect was running away so quickly that the witness cannot make a positive identification?

Investigators may then show the witness a book of mug shots of known criminals. While the witness may see someone who looks like the murderer, looking at mug shots limits the search only to those persons who have criminal records. The killer may have been someone who has no criminal record. To broaden the search, the witness may be asked to work with a police artist

A collection of sketches by Houston Police Department sketch artist Lois Gibson alongside the suspects' booking mug shots on display. Gibson's sketches have helped authorities catch hundreds of suspects. *David J. Phillip/AP*

who tries to create a sketch of the suspect based on the witness's description. With a wide menu of computerized facial features to choose from, a witness can often guide a police artist to draw a fairly accurate likeness of the suspect.

♀ PSYCHOLOGICAL PROFILING

In 1978 the FBI set up the first Psychological Profiling Program to help them in certain types of murder investigations. Psychological profiling was especially useful in serial murders, which seemed to be the work of someone with a severe psychological illness. Working with psychologists, the FBI tried to put together a personality profile of the killer. They sifted through the evidence from the crime scene to provide clues to the character of the murderer, such as age, gender, race, lifestyle, type of psychological illness, and motive for the crime.

The FBI profiling system breaks down offenders into organized and disorganized. The organized murderers plan their crimes in every detail and try to ensure that there is no evidence at the scene to involve them. The disorganized murderers do not plan their crimes and are more likely to act on the spur of the moment and leave far more evidence at the scene. The two types of murderers are divided by personality characteristics that include the following:

Organized	Disorganized
Average to above-average intelligence	Below-average intelligence
Socially competent	Socially inadequate
Skilled worker	Unskilled worker
Inconsistent discipline as child	Harsh discipline as child
Controlled mood during crime	Anxious mood during crime
Using alcohol with crime	Minimal use of alcohol
Living with partner	Living alone
Mobility with car	Lives/works near crime scene

(continues)

(continued)

According to author Wayne Petherick, "The FBI's method remains one of the most widely taught methods in the world." However, some experts disagree with the FBI's breakdown of types of killers. David Cantor, an investigative psychologist at the University of Liverpool, points out that serial killers fall into both categories—organized and disorganized. For example, they conceal a victim's body (an organized behavior), but may also mutilate a victim (a disorganized behavior).[3]

Police then circulate this sketch in the neighborhood and often on the TV news and in newspapers. Police may eventually track down a murder suspect. But once they find the suspect, investigators must check his alibi for the time when the murder was committed, his motive for committing the murder, as well as link him to evidence found at the homicide scene.

WORK OF THE CRIME LAB

Technicians in the modern crime laboratory perform much of the work of examining evidence that eventually leads to arrests. According to authors Charles Swanson, Neil Chamelin, and Leonard Territo, the crime lab technicians assist in this process "by answering, or helping to answer, the vital question of whether a crime has been committed, how and when it was committed, who committed it, and, just as important, who could not have committed it."[4] This effort begins at the scene of the crime, where evidence has been collected. Then it continues in the crime lab with the analysis of the evidence.

Perhaps the most widely publicized work of the crime lab involves blood testing. Blood samples may be found on the victim's clothes or in other areas of the crime scene. Lab technicians, known as serologists, carefully remove these samples and run tests on the blood. Adding water to tiny samples, serologists determine whether the blood is from a human or an animal. Serologists also test for blood type, which can be Type A, B, AB, or O. Most Americans are Type A or O; Types AB and B are far less common. By analyzing the type of the blood sample that may have been left by the murderer, investigators can narrow their search for the killer. Although blood grouping may help in an investigation, it is not done as much as in the past because a new form of testing can provide better results.

Much of the work performed by the serologists involves the analysis of Deoxyribonucleic Acid (DNA). Located in the nucleus of most body cells, a person's DNA contains the genetic code that gives each of us our individual characteristics. In fact, each person—with the exception of identical twins—has a unique set of DNA molecules.

Tiny bits of DNA can be extracted from blood, hair follicles, urine, semen, and saliva found at the crime scene. The saliva, for example, may be extracted from a piece of gum or a cigar that was found at the scene. Serologists use chemicals called enzymes to remove the DNA from the tiny sample and cut it into pieces. Different lengths of DNA are run through a fine gel, and the longer pieces are preserved because these are unique to each individual. These pieces become markers that are used to create a match between DNA from the crime scene and the DNA of a possible suspect.

Using nationwide databases, technicians look for a match between a sample in the computer system and the DNA sample from the homicide scene. One sequence of markers in a sample is not sufficient to create a match. Instead, the sequence must appear over and over again in the samples. These repeated sequences are called "short tandem repeat."

This process can help lead investigators to a suspect as long as DNA is found at the scene that belongs to the murderer and he or she is in the database. This may not happen. Even with DNA testing, investigators still rely on fingerprint identification to help them track down suspects. As Stan Lipinski, a California detective, put it, "Criminals don't leave prints or DNA deliberately—that's the important thing to realize. But, if you play the percentages, they're more likely to accidentally touch something at the scene than they are to bleed or sneeze . . . over the same item."[5] Some fingerprints have already been collected from the crime scene. Others may be revealed on evidence that is placed inside fuming chambers and heated with cyanoacrylate in the crime lab.

Fingerprints from the crime scene are examined for their patterns. These include loops, whorls, and arches. Depending on the pattern, a numerical value is assigned to the print from each finger. The total of these values from all the individual's prints can be entered into a large database called the Automated Fingerprint Identification System (AFIS). According to author John Houde, this yields "a list of likely suspects. . . . And each is manually checked [under a microscope] against the sample from the crime scene."[6] This enables fingerprint examiners to make comparisons and produces a likely match.

In addition to fingerprints and blood samples, the crime lab looks at trace evidence, such as pieces of glass, seeds, pollen, fibers, and hairs. In one case, a teacher's wife had been murdered as part of what appeared to have been a burglary. A crime scene technician examined the scene of the crime as part of the murder investigation. Among the things he found were pieces of a broken soda bottle. Later, two suspects were caught, and their car was seized and carefully searched. After thoroughly vacuuming the automobile to find any clues, a small piece of bottle glass was discovered. It physically matched the pieces of glass found at the crime scene. Using these pieces, the forensic technician had rebuilt the soda bottle except for the one piece of glass found in the car, which fit the bottle exactly. The suspects were charged with murder and later told investigators that they had been hired by the woman's husband to kill her and make it look like a burglary.

Under the microscope, fibers left at the scene of the crime can be carefully analyzed to determine where they came from. A carpet fiber made of nylon, for example, has a different shape from one manufactured from cotton or wool. Dust collected from the scene is examined to determine whether it came from another location. A match with the dust from a suspected murderer's living room may prove to be an important clue. An analysis of hairs can reveal which part of the body they came from. Examination of a round hair follicle from a suspected murderer's head, for example, will show its color and whether it was dyed. If the hair has been ripped out in a fight, pieces of skin attached to the hair will become evident under the microscope.

CAUSES OF MURDER

Homicides are committed by a variety of means, including poison or other drugs, knives, and firearms. In 1975 the body of a woman named Sophie Friedgood was discovered in her bedroom in Nassau County, New York. Dr. Leslie Lukash, the medical examiner of Nassau County, investigated the death. According to an article in the *New York Times*, "Dr. Lukash became suspicious when her

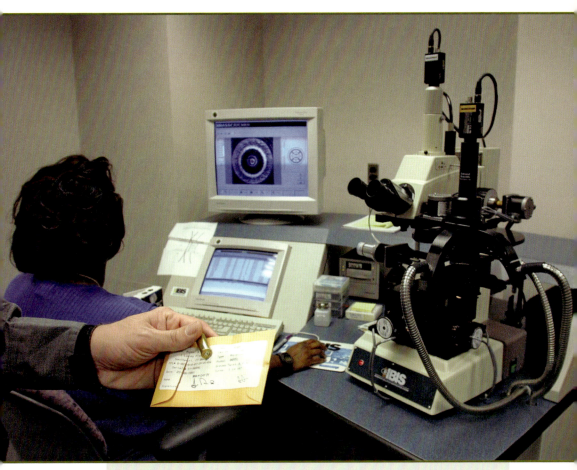

A New York State technical sergeant holds a shell casing at the New York State Police lab while a senior lab tech operates the equipment that looks for the markings on the casing, which identify the gun.
Jim McKnight/AP

husband, Dr. Charles Friedgood, signed the death certificate and sent the body to Pennsylvania for autopsy," and soon afterward Mrs. Friedgood was buried.[7] After examining tissue samples from the body before it was buried, Dr. Lukash concluded that Mrs. Friedgood had been killed with Demerol, a powerful painkiller. He then convinced the authorities in Pennsylvania to dig up the body. He found needle marks on her arm where the painkiller had been injected. Her husband was arrested and later found guilty of murder.

The majority of homicides, however, are committed with firearms—handguns, rifles, or shotguns. The projectiles from a firearm may be pellets or slugs fired by a shotgun, or a single bullet fired by a rifle or handgun. A gun fires when the firing pin strikes the cartridge and drives a bullet down the gun barrel as the gunpowder in the cartridge explodes. The cartridge includes a metal jacket, or case, surrounding a piece of metal called a bullet. Although the killer may not leave the murder weapon, bullets from a handgun or rifle may be found in the victim's body and perhaps in areas of the crime scene.

ARSON TO COVER UP A MURDER

Among the equipment found in the crime lab is the gas chromatograph (GC). A GC is a piece of equipment that a technician uses to analyze evidence collected from a crime scene to determine its component chemical parts. Each chemical is recorded as a different line on a graph. The GC can be especially useful in detecting chemicals such as gasoline that may have been used to start a fire. The gasoline may be found during the analysis of a piece of carpet found at the scene. The fire may have been started by a killer to cover up a homicide and make it look like an accident. In addition, an examination of the body during autopsy may reveal that there was no smoke in the victim's lungs. This indicates that the victim was dead before the fire started. In one case, the wife of a firefighter was found burned to death in the couple's home. An examination of the body revealed that no carbon dioxide had entered her lungs and there was no soot in her nose. This indicated that she had been dead before the fire started. Her husband later confessed to killing her.[8]

At the crime lab, ballistics experts begin with an examination of these bullets. A technician can determine the gun's caliber—the size of the inside of the barrel—from examining the bullet. The gun may be a .38, for example, indicating a barrel that is 38/100 of an inch in diameter. As the bullet is shot through the gun barrel, grooves on the inside of the barrel leave distinctive marks on the slug. These grooves can help identify the weapon and its manufacturer. If a cartridge case is found at the crime scene, it can also serve as valuable evidence. When a gun is fired, the firing pin leaves a distinctive mark on the back of the cartridge case that helps to identify the firearm.

With this information, a ballistics expert can use a huge firearm database to look for possible matches with similar slugs and cartridges used in other crimes. An early FBI database was called Drugfire, but the Integrated Ballistic Identification System (IBIS) later replaced it in 2002.

Sometimes a pistol or rifle is found at a crime scene, and ballistics experts must determine whether it was the weapon used in the homicide. They test the firearm by shooting it into a container of water. According to author Richard Platt, each bullet has "marks that are as unique as a human fingerprint. . . . To compare these scratches and grooves with those on the bullet recovered from the crime scene, or body of a victim, the examiner uses a comparison microscope. This enables the examiner to look at both bullets at once to compare them. A match is positive proof that the same gun fired both bullets."[9]

Using the Evidence to Convict a Suspect

Ellen and Edward Sherman were married on Long Island, outside New York City, in 1969. A short time after the wedding, the Shermans moved to Niantic, Connecticut, located along the shoreline. Edward Sherman had been hired to teach marketing at Mohegan Community College. The couple also ran a successful company called Ad Graphics, which published the *Showcase of Homes*, a magazine that displayed houses for sale in the region where they lived. Ellen Sherman was especially proud of her work at Ad Graphics, where she made a substantial income. The couple had one child, a little girl named Janice.

There were many reasons for Ellen and Edward Sherman to enjoy their life together, but problems soon arose in their marriage. Edward began having relationships with other women, one of whom worked with him at Mohegan Community College. Ellen also became romantically involved with other men, including Len Fredrickson, one of her coworkers at Ad Graphics.

By 1985 Ellen and Edward were seriously considering divorce, after his latest girlfriend became pregnant with his child. She wanted Edward to leave his wife and marry her. Meanwhile, Ellen told her husband that she had become pregnant with the couple's second child, and she demanded that Edward leave his girlfriend. On June 16, 1985, the Shermans engaged in a particularly nasty fight that lasted the entire day. Edward threw some of the couple's furniture around the living room and beat his wife. The next day, when Ellen appeared at her office for work, she was wearing sunglasses and makeup, probably to cover up her bruises.

Following the argument, Edward Sherman moved out of the couple's home and began living on their boat. Soon afterward, however, Edward apparently had a change of heart, and promised his wife that he would give up the relationship with his girlfriend and try to patch up their marriage. He moved back into their home and, according to one of the couple's friends, Ellen and Edward were "acting like newlyweds."[1]

This proved to be only a temporary calm before an even wilder storm. By July 1985 Ellen realized that her husband was still seeing his girlfriend, and she resumed her efforts to seek a divorce. Since she owned a larger part of Ad Graphics than her husband, Ellen told her friends, "I can take care of myself and our children." She also planned to keep the business and their house, and "leave him with nothing."[2] Yet, for some reason, Ellen decided not to go through with the divorce. Instead, she was determined to give her marriage to Edward one more chance.

Edward Sherman planned to leave on a sailing trip with some of his friends on August 2, 1985. They were going to pick up a boat in Maine and sail it along the coast to Connecticut. That morning, Ellen gave her husband a special card for his 42nd birthday. They spent part of the day together at a nearby swimming pool and came back home in the afternoon. Ellen was seen walking their dog shortly afterward and then returned inside the house.

Later that afternoon, Edward Sherman drove his car up the street and pulled over to have a conversation with his neighbors, Charles VonKrack and his wife. They thought that this behavior was quite unusual because Sherman had never spoken to them before, although they had all lived in the same neighborhood for several years. Earlier that day, Sherman had a telephone conversation with the daughter of one of his sailing friends. He asked if she had seen a recent movie on television, entitled *Blackout* (1985), in which a husband murders his wife and then turns on the air conditioning in the room where the homicide had occurred to preserve the body and mask the time of death.

Around 7:30 p.m., Sherman was picked up by one of the men accompanying him on the sailing trip. The man later explained that he thought it was unusual that Ellen Sherman did not come out to say goodbye to her husband. The two men stopped to pick up the other men who were going on the trip. At the home of Bill Albright, Sherman said that he wanted to call Ellen to discuss a few matters before he left for Maine. While Edward was talking on the telephone, the Albright's eight-year-old daughter, Jamie, was listening in on the conversation. "If you need anything, go to the neighbors," Jamie heard him say." Then Sherman added, "Goodbye, honey. . . . I love you, too."[3] Later, Jamie said that she had not heard anybody on the other end of the line while Sherman was talking.

The next day, when Sherman and his friends were out at sea, he made more calls to his wife using the ship's radio. Sherman told his friends that he was unable to reach her. Nevertheless, he continued putting in calls, and becoming more and more concerned when he received no answer. Finally, Sherman radioed a neighbor and asked her to check on Ellen. Instead, the neighbor sent Len Frederickson, Ellen's coworker, over to the Sherman house on Sunday night.

When he arrived in front of the Sherman home, Frederickson saw that the shades were drawn and didn't see any sign of life inside. Eventually he pushed open a screen in one of the windows and let himself inside. The house was completely dark and quiet, and there was no sign of Ellen Sherman or anyone else. Frederickson walked through the downstairs of the house and then climbed the stairway to the second floor. He slowly opened the door to the Shermans' bedroom, and there he saw Ellen Sherman's body lying on the bed. The air conditioner in the room was running at high speed and had turned the room into a frigid tomb.

HOMICIDE INVESTIGATION

Frederickson called police and they arrived at the crime scene a short time later. Frederickson had left the door to the master bedroom open, and much of the cool air had escaped. Dr. Henry C. Lee, the chief criminologist for Connecticut and a renowned forensic expert, was among the investigators who arrived at the Sherman home. As Lee began to examine the body, he noticed that there were marks on Ellen Sherman's throat. Using a magnifying glass, Lee carefully studied the body and the other evidence in the bedroom.

One important piece of evidence was the victim's panties. Lee later wrote: "I recognized a pattern in the elastic band which went around the wearer's waist, and I compared this to the pattern I had observed on the victim's neck. . . . They were very similar."[4] Lee thought that Ellen Sherman might have been strangled with the panties. But he noticed other marks on Ellen Sherman's neck,

Renowned forensic scientist Henry C. Lee, a chief investigator in the
Ellen Sherman murder, testifies in the Phil Spector murder trial in
2007. *Paul Buck/epa/Corbis*

indicating that the killer had also used his or her hands to strangle
Ellen. There were also marks that might have come from the victim's saliva on the sheets, suggesting that she had been strangled
while lying face down.

   One of the most confusing pieces of evidence at the crime scene
was the condition of the body. The victim still showed signs of rigor
mortis, which usually begins two to four hours after death occurs,
starts disappearing after one and one half days, and then completely

vanishes in two and one half days. Since the rigor mortis was still present, this suggested that Ellen Sherman had been killed less than two days earlier.

Dr. Catherine Galvin, another medical examiner, arrived at the murder scene and also examined the body. She believed that, because the rigor mortis was still present, death had occurred some time between 10 p.m. on Friday, August 2, and soon after sunrise on Sunday, August 4.

From the beginning, police had considered Edward Sherman a prime suspect in the case. Interviews with witnesses revealed that the marriage had been tumultuous and that Ellen Sherman had threatened to divorce Edward, take their business, and leave him with nothing. However, if the murder had not occurred until at least 10 p.m. on August 2, Edward Sherman had an airtight alibi: He had been with his friends traveling to Maine. Dr. Lee disagreed with Dr. Galvin's assessment. He believed that the cold temperatures caused by the air-conditioning had prevented the rigor mortis from disappearing and reduced the amount of decomposition in the body. Lee thought that death could have occurred earlier, giving Sherman time to commit the homicide before he had left on his trip.

An autopsy of Ellen Sherman's body later revealed something else: The contents of her stomach, a pasta dinner, were still present. This indicated that she had eaten dinner no more than five hours before her murder and would be inconsistent with a time of death as late as the one suggested by Dr. Galvin.

Although police brought Edward Sherman in for questioning, there was not enough evidence to indicate that he might be guilty of the homicide. Police did not obtain a warrant to search the Sherman house until almost a week after the murder. While they found leftovers from the pasta dinner inside the refrigerator, Sherman's lawyers argued that these could have been placed there after the murder to cast suspicion on their client. Although Sherman did not seem very upset over his wife's death, this was not enough to charge him with murder.

After Ellen's funeral, Sherman moved in with his girlfriend. Later he inherited more than $200,000 from his wife's will. Police believed that these developments provided additional motives for Sherman to have committed the murder. They refused to give up on the case, and finally in 1990 Edward Sherman was arrested and charged with murder.

attentions had turned to a new man named Paul Solomon, a sixth-grade teacher. Solomon and his wife, Betty Jeanne, lived a short distance away from the elementary school. Warmus and Solomon soon began a passionate relationship. Carolyn began visiting the couple's home and even befriended their daughter Kristan, a student at the local high school. She bought Kristan expensive gifts and even took her on a skiing trip to Vermont.

Although Carolyn wanted Solomon to leave his wife, he refused and finally ended their relationship in the middle of 1988. But Warmus would not accept Solomon's decision, and eventually she convinced him to resume their affair. Early in 1989 Warmus arranged to buy a gun from a private detective named Vincent Parco. Parco was an old friend, and he may have been involved in a romantic relationship with Warmus. Parco contacted a gun maker named George Peters and paid him to fit a Beretta pistol with a silencer, which Parco then sold to Warmus for $2,500.

On Sunday, January 15, 1989, Warmus called Solomon at his home and arranged to meet him for dinner at a nearby restaurant. Solomon told his wife that he was going out to meet some friends for their regular bowling night and left the house about 6:30 p.m. About 45 minutes later, a 911 operator received a frantic call from a woman at the Solomon home. The caller said, "he" or "she is trying to kill me."[9] Then the line went dead.

Meanwhile, Solomon had arrived at the restaurant, but he did not see Warmus anywhere inside. Eventually, she joined him for dinner at about 7:45 p.m. Following the meal, which ended at about 10:30 p.m., Solomon returned to his home. Once inside, he saw the television was on in the living room and, mysteriously, his wife seemed to be sleeping on the floor. Solomon tried to awaken her, but Betty Jeanne did not respond. When he turned his wife over on her back, Solomon realized that she had been shot and was dead.

THE INVESTIGATION

After detectives arrived at the Solomon home and began examining the scene of the homicide, they discovered six .25-caliber shell casings. Nothing had been stolen, nor had any of the doors or windows been forced open. So the police concluded that Betty Jeanne Solomon had not been a victim of a burglary. Indeed, they believed that she had probably been acquainted with the murderer and had let him or her into the house. Their attention immediately turned to her husband, Paul Solomon. But Solomon claimed that he had been at the bowling lanes with his friends. After questioning, however, Solomon finally admitted spending some of the evening with his girlfriend, Carolyn Warmus. Police wondered if Solomon had killed his wife so he could marry Warmus. They then visited Warmus, who backed up Solomon's alibi that he had been with her.

While Solomon was sure that he had not committed the murder, he was not so sure about Carolyn Warmus. Soon after his wife's funeral, he asked her, "Did you have anything to do with Betty Jeanne's death?"

Warmus answered, "Paul, I'm so glad you feel comfortable enough to ask me that. No, I would never do anything to hurt you

Exterior view of the two-story apartment complex where Carolyn Warmus shot Paul Solomon's wife before meeting him at a restaurant. *Michael Abramson/Time & Life Pictures/Getty Images*

or Kristan."[10] Nevertheless, Solomon's feelings for Warmus had cooled, and he began a relationship with another woman named Barbara Ballor. This infuriated Warmus, who wanted Solomon for herself.

In an effort to put an end to the relationship, Warmus called Ballor's parents. Saying she was a police detective, she told them

THE MATHISON CASE AND BLOOD SPATTER EVIDENCE

Kenneth Mathison was a highly respected police officer who lived with his wife, Yvonne, and their children in the Hilo area of Hawaii. On November 27, 1992, the Mathisons were driving in their van through a heavy rain when Kenneth told his wife that he had been having a relationship with another woman who was now pregnant. Yvonne Mathison was so upset that she stopped the van, got out, and began walking along the busy highway. A passing motorist saw Mrs. Mathison. Later, two retired policemen saw a man with a woman's body in the back of a van parked on the side of the road.

Following a 911 call to police, investigators arrived at the scene and found the dead body of Yvonne Mathison in the back of the van. Kenneth Mathison told police that his wife had left the van following an argument and as he drove through the heavy rain looking for her, he had accidentally run over Yvonne and killed her. He told police that he had then carried her body back to the van. At first he put it in the front seat but then later moved it to the back where he secured the body with yellow rope.

An autopsy of Yvonne Mathison's body revealed that she had suffered bruises to the head, hand, and arms that might have been caused when she was struck by the van. Her death was considered an accident and her body was cremated at her husband's request.

Assistant District Attorney Kurt W. Spohn, however, was not satisfied with the finding and ordered further investigation. Photos from inside the van showed blood spatter patterns that could have been caused when Kenneth Mathison put his wife's body into the van. But at least one bloodstain pattern on the instrument panel looked as if it could have resulted from an external blow to about Solomon, explaining that he was suspected of murdering his wife by shooting her eight times. They called their daughter and asked her about Solomon. Barbara then contacted the police, whose attention had turned to Carolyn Warmus as a suspect in the murder case. Since they had not released any information about the number of gunshots fired at the victim, they knew that only the murderer

the head that might have occurred inside the van. Examination of the van confirmed these early findings. In addition, Yvonne Mathison's blood and hair were found on the running board along the driver's side of the van. Further examination showed that the hair had been torn from her head after a blow to the left side. More blood spatter patterns were found on the roof inside the van, which appeared to have been caused by a blow to the victim.

As a result of this additional evidence, Kenneth Mathison was charged with the murder of his wife, Yvonne, on November 27, 1992. During the trial, Spohn pointed out that Mathison had business interests that had put him in debt for almost $1 million. He had also taken out a large life insurance policy on his wife. In addition, Mathison had lied to the insurance company by saying that he was a nonsmoker, which meant he paid a lower premium rate for the insurance policy, when, in fact, he did smoke cigarettes.

Dr. Werner Spitz, a forensic pathologist, testified that photos of Yvonne Mathison's body taken during the autopsy showed bruises to her head that had to have been made by a weapon. "This was a perpendicular blow," Dr. Spitz said, which came from above and could not have been caused when she was hit by an automobile.[13] The blood spatter evidence confirmed Spitz's testimony. In addition, a neighbor named Laurie Raquel testified about a fight between Yvonne and Kenneth Mathison a month before the highway death. Although Mathison tried to explain away all of this evidence, the jury did not believe him. Blood spatter evidence and eyewitness testimony convinced the jury and they found him guilty of murder. Mathison was sentenced to life in prison.

could be aware of this information. Meanwhile, police had obtained a court order for Warmus's telephone records and uncovered her connection to Vincent Parco.

Warmus had a motive to kill Betty Jeanne Solomon and had enough time to kill her before she arrived at the restaurant, but there was still no way to link Warmus to the murder weapon. Then a former business associate of Vincent Parco who had heard about the case contacted police. He said that Parco had arranged for George Peters to fit a Beretta (gun) with a silencer. A search of Peters' workshop revealed a bullet and a shell casing produced when Peters had tested the gun. Careful examination of the casing in the crime lab revealed that it matched those discovered at the murder scene. Soon afterward, Warmus was arrested and charged with murder.

THE TRIALS

Carolyn Warmus's trial began on January 14, 1991. Prosecutor James McCarty put a long line of witnesses on the stand, each of whom described Warmus's relationship with Paul Solomon. Not only did she have a motive, Warmus also had the opportunity, McCarty explained, to kill Betty Jeanne. She could have done it between the time that Solomon left his home and the time that Warmus arrived at the restaurant. Her telephone records also indicated that she had called a sporting goods shop, where a woman with a fake driver's license, but matching Warmus's description, had purchased .25-caliber shells.

In response to the charges against his client, Warmus's attorney, David Lewis, claimed that Solomon and Parco had engineered the murder. Carolyn Warmus was only guilty of having a relationship with a married man. "We must be careful not to be swayed in our moral judgment . . . of a young girl in this day and age," Lewis said.[11] Lewis also pointed out that the police had mishandled the evidence at the crime scene: A glove that was visible in a police photograph had mysteriously disappeared from the murder scene. In addition, police had permitted Paul Solomon to clean his wife's blood from his hands after arriving at the scene, which may have helped him cover up his involvement in the crime.

After weeks of testimony, the jury retired to consider the evidence. Following a long deliberation, they could not unanimously agree on a verdict—that is, they were a hung jury. In a murder trial, a guilty verdict must be unanimous. With a hung jury, Carolyn Warmus was freed. The police were dissatisfied with the outcome of the trial and continued their investigation. Eventually, Paul Solomon found the missing glove inside a closet at his home. According to the editors of *Crimes of Passion,* "An electron microscope . . . revealed faint bloodstains in the shape of fingertips on the back of the glove, as if a bloody hand had grasped it. Moreover, a match was made between the glove and fibers found under Betty Jeanne Solomon's fingernails." This suggested a struggle between the victim and her murderer. A check of Carolyn Warmus's credit card records showed that she had purchased gloves "that proved a match to the mystery glove in material, style, and manufacturer." Kristan Solomon then told police that the glove was "almost exactly like the pair" Warmus had loaned her on their skiing trip to Vermont.[12]

This new evidence and the work of the crime lab were enough to convict Carolyn Warmus at her second trial, and she was sentenced to 25 years to life in prison.

The Scales of Justice:
New Evidence Frees Convicted Murderers

In August 1980 Lindy and Michael Chamberlain took a family camping trip near Ayers Rock in Australia's Northern Territory. As they were preparing dinner, they saw a wild dog—known as a dingo—leaving the tent where their two young children had been resting. Lindy reached the tent as the dingo disappeared into the brush and discovered that their infant daughter, Azaria, was gone.

When police arrived at the scene, they found blood inside the tent and began searching for the dingo and the Chamberlain's baby girl. Eventually, some of the child's clothes were discovered, but her body was never found. Police were suspicious of Lindy Chamberlain's story that a dingo had taken her child. "There were no bite marks or dingo saliva on Azaria's romper, but there were cuts and bloodstains. . . . Dingoes just didn't take children," according to police.[1]

Nevertheless, there was no hard evidence to indicate that Lindy or her husband had killed the baby. At an inquest—an official hearing on the case held by a coroner—the dingo was officially blamed for the death. The Australian media, however, was not willing to accept the verdict, nor did the Australian police stop their investigation. They found a "bloody print in the shape of a woman's hand"[2] on the baby's clothes, according to author Richard Platt. Further investigation revealed a pair of scissors with bloodstains in the

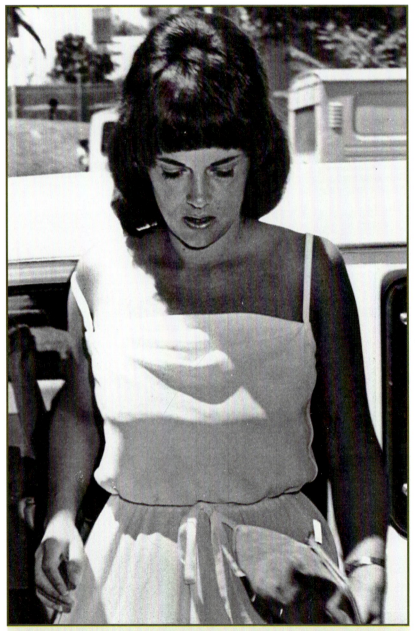

Lindy Chamberlain at the Alice Springs Court House in February 1982.
She was convicted for the murder of her nine-week-old daughter,
Azaria. Four years later, new evidence was discovered and she was
exonerated and released. *AP*

Chamberlain's car, and police concluded that the cuts in Azaria's clothes could have been made by the scissors.

In 1982 Lindy Chamberlain was arrested for the murder of her daughter. After listening to the evidence presented at her trial, a jury found Mrs. Chamberlain guilty of murder, and she was sentenced to a long prison term at hard labor. Then, four years later, new evidence was discovered: Azaria's jacket was discovered near the crime scene and it appeared that a dingo had buried it. The blood in the car, after more careful testing, turned out not to be blood but another substance (the testing was not done carefully enough in the original investigation). Finally, according to Platt, a report by a Royal Commission "concluded that the bloodstains and marks on the romper were consistent with a dingo attack after all."[3] As a result, Lindy Chamberlain was freed from prison.

EVIDENCE IS NOT ALWAYS WHAT IT SEEMS

As compelling as evidence may seem in a homicide investigation, the police can make mistakes. Since 1989, according to *USA Today*, 328 defendants convicted of homicide or rape have been freed when new evidence was discovered or existing evidence was re-evaluated.[4] In part, this is due to advancements in DNA identification, which permits police to match blood, hair, or semen found at the scene of the crime with that of a convicted prisoner.

Many of these defendants had been convicted based on eyewitness testimony. But an eyewitness who catches only a fleeting glimpse of a murderer following a homicide can easily make a mistake when looking at a police lineup or at an individual's mug shot. In some cases, a suspect confesses to a crime after hours and hours of interrogation by police. But the false confession may occur just because the suspect is exhausted and willing to admit to a crime simply to end the interrogation. In other cases, a witness may lie on the witness stand (commit perjury) out of revenge. Or a witness who has been convicted of a crime may have agreed to provide testimony in return for having his or her sentence reduced.

In 2007 Timothy Atkins was freed from prison after 20 years behind bars. In 1987 Atkins was accused of murdering Vincente Gonzalez, based on eyewitness testimony. Gonzalez's wife, Maria, stated that she had been walking with her husband when two men approached them. One of the men, she said, was Atkins, although she only saw him briefly. According to law professor Gerald Uelmen, Executive Director of the California Commission on the Fair Administration of Justice, "Eyewitness misidentification is the leading cause of wrongful convictions across the country."[5] Atkins was also convicted because another inmate named Marvin Moore provided testimony against him. Moore said that Atkins had told him in jail that he had been at the scene of the murder and, in return, Moore was released from jail. Finally, a woman named Denise Powell said that she had heard Atkins tell a friend that he had committed the murder.

Since there was no blood from the homicide scene that could be linked to the murderer, Atkins' attorneys relied on other means to finally secure his release. Powell said that she had been mistaken and changed her testimony. Maria Gonzalez's identification turned out to be incorrect. And Moore also changed his story.

Not only can witness testimony be faulty, but other types of evidence can also be unreliable in a homicide investigation. Lisa Faber runs the hair-and-fiber investigation team for the New York City Police Department. In a recent murder case involving the deaths of two policemen, she examined fibers found on the clothes of the suspected murderer. The prosecution was trying to prove that he had been in the automobile where the police officers were killed. After close examination, the best Faber could say was that the fibers "could have originated" from the car. She added, "The strongest association you can say is that 'it could have come from' a specific crime scene."[6] Faber added, "We never use the word 'match.' The terminology is very important. On TV, they always like to say words like 'match,' but we say 'similar,' or 'could have come from,' or 'is associated with.'"[7]

Margaret A. Berger, a professor at Brooklyn Law School, points out, "We know from a lot of DNA exonerations [reversing convictions and freeing prisoners] that they come from bad hair evidence."[8] In a rape case in 1987 hairs found at the crime scene were linked to a suspect, Jimmy Ray Bromgard, and he was convicted of the crime. But in 2002 DNA testing of sperm from the victim's clothing proved that he was not guilty.[9]

As a result of improvements in DNA testing, courts rely more heavily on it to provide the most reliable evidence for major crimes, such as rape and murder. This can be performed on blood, semen, and hair. In 2006 Jeffrey Mark Deskovic was released from prison after being convicted 16 years earlier of the murder of a high school student. Prior to his conviction, Deskovic had been interrogated by police for six hours and finally confessed to the murder. "I was tired, confused, scared, hungry—I wanted to get out of there. I told the police what they wanted to hear, but I never got to go home."[10] DNA testing was in its early stages in 1990 and not very reliable. It seemed to show that Deskovic was not guilty of the crime, but the jury chose to believe his confession. New tests finally revealed a match with someone else, a criminal currently in prison for murder.

DNA evidence was also used to free Dennis Halstead, convicted of killing Theresa Fusco in 1984. Halstead had been found guilty based on the testimony of John Kogut, who had told police after 18 hours of questioning that he and another man had been with Halstead, who had committed the murder. DNA tests conducted during the 1990s and in 2001 proved that someone else, not Halstead, had committed the murder. Due to the work of Halstead's lawyers, he was released from prison in 2003.

In the twenty-first century, homicide investigators have far more tools at their fingertips than detectives had in the past. These tools enable police to examine crime scenes more carefully, collect more evidence, analyze it more thoroughly, and catch many of the criminals who have committed homicide. Nevertheless, they can still make mistakes. As a result, prosecutors, police, and juries must weigh evidence very carefully before any person is charged with or convicted of homicide.

Chronology

c. 1760 B.C.	Code of Hammurabi developed.
44 B.C.	Julius Caesar murdered.
1170 A.D.	Thomas Becket murdered.
1740s	Henry Fielding organizes the Bow Street Runners in London.
1829	First paid professional police force formed in London.
1841	Mary Rogers murdered.
1845	First paid professional police force in United States formed in New York City.
1847	Duchess Choiseul-Praslin murdered.
1857	Duncan Skinner murdered.
1880s	Ballistic testing begins.
1888	Psychological profiling begins.
1892	Francis Galton publishes a book on fingerprint identification.
1906	Stanford White murdered.
1910	Belle Crippen murdered.
1923	August Vollmer sets up model crime laboratory in Berkeley, California.
1978	Jack Tupper murdered; FBI sets up Psychological Profiling Program.
1980	Dr. Herman Tarnower murdered.
1985	Margaret Benson murdered; Ellen Sherman murdered; DNA testing begins.
1986	Juan Gonzales kills passengers on Staten Island Ferry.
1989	Betty Jeanne Solomon murdered.
1992	Yvonne Mathison murdered.
1994	Nicole Simpson murdered.
1999	Massacre at Columbine High School.
2007	Massacre at Virginia Tech University.

Endnotes

Introduction

1. Sharon Begley, "The Anatomy of Violence," *Newsweek*, April 30, 2007, 46.

Chapter 1

1. "The Assassination of Julius Caesar, 44 BC." EyeWitness-toHistory.com. http://www.eyewitnesstohistory.com/pfcaesar2.htm. Accessed on March 5, 2007.
2. Ibid.
3. "The Murder of Thomas Becket, 1170." EyeWitness-toHistory.com. http://www.eyewitnesstohistory.com/pfbecket.htm. Accessed on March 5, 2007.
4. Ibid.
5. Time-Life Editors, *Crimes of Passion.* (London: Treasure Press, 1984), 60.
6. Ibid., 62.
7. Michael Wayne, *Death of an Overseer* (New York: Oxford University Press, 2001), 9.
8. Troy Taylor, "The Girl in the Red Velvet Swing," Prairie Ghosts. http://www.prairieghosts.com/thaw.html. Accessed on March 5, 2007.

Chapter 2

1. Begley, "The Anatomy of Violence," 46.
2. Ibid.

3. Bureau of Justice Statistics, Homicide Trends. http://www.ojp.usdoj.gov/bjs/homicide/hmrt.htm. Accessed March 12, 2008.
4. Ibid.
5. David Owen, *Hidden Evidence* (Buffalo, N.Y.: Firefly Books, 2000), 65.
6. Ibid., 99.
7. Ibid., 138.
8. Time-Life Editors, *True Crime: Crimes of Passion* (Alexandria, Va.: Time-Life Books, 1994), 45–46.
9. Ibid., 84–85.
10. Begley, "The Anatomy of Violence," 43.
11. Ibid., 42.
12. Ibid., 42

Chapter 3

1. "Policing in London before the Bobbies," *The Proceedings of the Old Bailey.* http://www.oldbaileyonline.org/history/crime/policing.html. Accessed on August 6, 2007.
2. Ibid.
3. Gavan Tredoux, "Henry Faulds: The Invention of a Finger-printer," December 2003. http://galton.org/fingerprints/faulds.htm. Accessed on January 10, 2008.

4. Edward Ricciuti, *Science 101: Forensics* (New York: Harper-Collins, 2007), 12.
5. Barbara Conklin, et al., *Encyclopedia of Forensic Science* (Westport, Conn.: Oryx Press, 2002), 72–74.
6. "Talk with Former FBI Profiler John Douglas," CNN Live Today, October 25, 2002. http://transcripts.cnn.com/TRANSCRIPTS/0210/25/lt.06.html. Accessed on January 10, 2008.
7. Frank Smyth, *Cause of Death: The Story of Forensic Science* (New York: Van Nostrand Reinhold, 1980), 28.
8. Ricciuti, *Science 101: Forensics*, 15.
9. Patricia Cline Cohen, *The Murder of Helen Jewett* (New York: Random House, 1999), 20.

Chapter 4

1. Richard Platt, *Crime Scene* (New York: DK Publishing, 2003), 24–25.
2. "Death Investigation: A Guide for the Scene Investigator," U.S. Department of Justice. http://www.ncjrs.gov/pdffiles/167568,pdf. Accessed on January 8, 2008.
3. Steven Staggs, *Crime Scene and Evidence Photographer's Guide*, Crime Scene Investigator. http://www.crime-scene-investigator.net/closeup.html. Accessed on August 10, 2007.
4. Owen, *Hidden Evidence*, 162–163.

5. Ricciuti, *Science 101: Forensics*, 24.
6. Owen, *Hidden Evidence*, 187.
7. N.E Genge, *The Forensic Casebook* (New York: Ballantine Books) 60–61.
8. George Schiro, "Bloodstain Photography," Crime Scene Investigator. http://www.crime-scene-investigator.net/phoblood.html. Accessed on August 10, 2007.
9. Louis Akin, "Blood Spatter Interpretation at Crime and Accident Scenes," *FBI Law Enforcement Bulletin*, February 2005.
10. Jessica Sachs, "Blood is the Ink, Crime is the Story," *Popular Science*, January 2004, 32–35.

Chapter 5

1. Vernon J. Geberth, *Practical Homicide Investigation* (Boca Raton, Fla.: CRC Press, 1996), 237.
2. Ibid., 216.
3. Ibid., 217.
4. Genge, *The Forensic Casebook*, 182.
5. Platt, *Crime Scene*, 38–39.
6. Alison Maxwell, "Forensic Sculptor Brings the Dead to Life," USATODAY.com. http://www.usatoday.com/careers/dream/2001-march-forensic-sculptor.html. Accessed on January 10, 2008.
7. Brendan Vaughan, "Frank Bender," *Esquire*, April 2004.

Chapter 6

1. Genge, *The Forensic Casebook*, 137.
2. John Houde, *Crime Lab: A Guide for Nonscientists* (Ventura, Cal.: Calico Press, 1999), 45.
3. Wayne Petherick, "The FBI's Crime Scene Analysis, *Crime Library.* http://www.crimelibrary.com/criminal_mind/profiling/profiling2/1.html. Accessed March 12, 2008.
4. Charles Swanson, Neil Chamelin, and Leonard Territo, *Criminal Investigation* (New York: McGraw-Hill, 1992), 229.
5. Genge, *The Forensic Casebook*, 57.
6. Houde, *Crime Lab: A Guide for Nonscientists*, 55.
7. Douglas Martin, "Leslie Lukash, Medical Examiner, 86, Dies," *New York Times*, August 25, 2007.
8. Martin, "Leslie Lukash, Medical Examiner, 86, Dies."
9. Platt, *Crime Scene*, 102.

Chapter 7

1. Henry C. Lee, *Cracking Cases: The Science of Solving Crimes* (Amherst, N.Y.: Prometheus Books, 2002), 237.
2. Ibid., 238.
3. Ibid., 241
4. Ibid., 245.
5. Ibid., 257.
6. Time-Life Editors, *True Crime: Crimes of Passion*, 52.

7. Ibid., 52.
8. Ibid., 59.
9. Ibid., 65.
10. Ibid., 69.
11. Ibid., 74.
12. Ibid., 78.
13. Lee, *Cracking Cases: The Science of Solving Crimes*, 47.

Chapter 8

1. Platt, *Crime Scene*, 64.
2. Ibid.
3. Ibid., 65.
4. "DNA Evidence Frees Falsely Accused," *USA Today*, March 2005. Available online. URL: http://www.truthinjustice.org/DNA-frees3.htm. Accessed on August 11, 2007.
5. Greg Moran, "Wrongly Convicted Man Walks Free After 2 Decades," *The San Diego Union-Tribune*, February 10, 2007.
6. Jeffrey Toobin, "The CSI Effect," *The New Yorker*, May 7, 2007, 31.
7. Ibid., 31.
8. Ibid., 34.
9. Fernanda Santos, "DNA Evidence Frees a Man Imprisoned for Half His Life," NYTimes.com. http://www.nytimes.com/2006/09/21/nyregion/21dna.html. Accessed on August 11, 2007.
10. Fernanda Santos, "Vindicated by DNA, But A Lost Man on the Outside," *New York Times*, November 25, 2007, p. 39.

Bibliography

Geberth, Vernon. *Practical Homicide Investigation*. Boca Raton, Fla.: CRC Press, 1996.

Genge, N.E. *The Forensic Casebook*. New York: Ballantine Books, 2002.

Houde, John. *Crime Lab: A Guide for Nonscientists*. Ventura, Calif.: Calico Press, 1999.

Lee, Henry. *Cracking Cases: The Science of Solving Crimes.* Amherst, N.Y.: Prometheus Books, 2002.

Owen, David. *Hidden Evidence: Forty True Crimes and How Forensic Science Helped Solve Them*. Buffalo, N.Y.: Firefly Books, 2000.

Platt, Richard. *Crime Scene*. New York: DK Publishing, 2003.

Ricciuti, Edward. *Science 101: Forensics*. New York: HarperCollins, 2007.

Smyth, Frank. *Cause of Death: The Story of Forensic Science*. New York: Van Nostrand Reinhold, 1980.

Further Resources

Books

Ferllini, Roxana. *Silent Witness: How Forensic Anthropology Is Used to Solve the World's Toughest Crimes*. Buffalo, N.Y.: Firefly Books, 2002.

Worth, Richard. *Children, Violence and Murder*. Philadelphia: Chelsea House, 2001.

Worth, Richard. *The Insanity Defense*. Philadelphia: Chelsea House, 2001.

Web Sites

Crime-Scene Investigation
http://www.crime-scene-investigator.net/

Federal Bureau of Investigation Publications
http://www.fbi.gov/publications.htm

Historic-UK.com
http://www.historic-uk.com

The Proceedings of the Old Bailey
http://www.oldbaileyonline.org/

U.S. Department of Justice—Office of Justice Programs, Bureau of Justice Statistics, Homicide Trends in U.S.
http://www.ojp.usdoj.gov/bjs/homicide/hmrt.htm

Index

Page numbers in *italics* indicate images.

About the Author

Richard Worth has 30 years of experience as a writer, trainer, and video producer. He has written more than 50 books. Many of his books are for young adults on topics that include family living, foreign affairs, biography, and history. He has written an eight-part radio series on Fiorello LaGuardia, which aired on National Public Radio. He also received the New York Public Library 2003 Best Books of the Teenage List award for *Gangs and Crime*, published by Chelsea House.

About the Consulting Editor

John L. French is a 31-year veteran of the Baltimore City Police Crime Laboratory. He is currently a crime laboratory supervisor. His responsibilities include responding to crime scenes, overseeing the preservation and collection of evidence, and training crime scene technicians. He has been actively involved in writing the operating procedures and technical manual for his unit and has conducted training in numerous areas of crime scene investigation. In addition to his crime scene work, Mr. French is also a published author, specializing in crime fiction. His short stories have appeared in *Alfred Hitchcock's Mystery Magazine* and numerous anthologies.